Financial Fitness for Life

Shaping Up Your Financial Future

Grades 6-8

Teacher Guide

Barbara Flowers
Sheryl Szot Gallaher

NCEE

National Council on Economic Education

Authors:

Barbara Flowers is the Assistant Director of the Center for Entrepreneurship and Economic Education at the University of Missouri-St. Louis. She has worked on numerous economic education publications.

Sheryl Szot Gallaher is the Director of the Office of Economic Education at Governors State University in University Park, Illinois. She was formerly a classroom teacher, Gifted Education Coordinator, and economic education consultant for the Illinois Council on Economic Education.

Project Director:

John E. Clow is the Director of the Leatherstocking Center for Economic Education at the State University of New York, College at Oneonta and Professor Emeritus of that college. He is a national award-winning college teacher, speaker, and author in the fields of personal finance, economics, and business education.

Design:
Roher/Sprague Partners

This publication was made possible through funding by the Bank of America Foundation.

ISBN 1-56183-544-7   5 4 3 2 1

TABLE OF CONTENTS

6–8

THEME 1:
There Is No Such Thing As a Free Lunch
(The Economic Way of Thinking)

THEME 2:
Education Pays Off: Learn Something
(Earning Income)

THEME 3:
Tomorrow's Money: Getting to the End of the Rainbow
(Saving)

THEME 4:
Spending and Credit Are Serious Business
(Spending and Using Credit)

THEME 5:
Get a Plan: Get a Grip on Life
(Money Management)

Lesson is appropriate for all students in 6–8 grade levels.

Lesson may be challenging for some students in grade 6.

Acknowledgements

The members of the writing team express their sincere appreciation to the many individuals who were involved with this project.

Reviewers:

Gwen Reichbach, *Executive Director*
National Institute for Consumer Education
Eastern Michigan University
Ypsilanti, Michigan

Kim Sosin, *Co-Director*
Center for Economic Education
University of Nebraska-Omaha
Omaha, Nebraska

State council directors who coordinated the field-testing:

R. J. (Jim) Charkins, California Council on Economic Education, San Bernardino, California

Donald G. Fell, Florida Council on Economic Education, Tampa, Florida

David L. Ramsour, Texas Council on Economic Education, Houston, Texas

Teachers, students, and parents involved in field-testing in California, Florida, and Texas.

General Editor:

Richard Western
Milwaukee, Wisconsin

Some materials were adapted from *Money in the Middle*, a 1996 publication of the National Council on Economic Education, by Raymond E. Forgue, Beth Randolph, and Mary Ann Farley. The publication was underwritten by a consortium of 10 Consumer Credit Counseling Services (CCCS) Agencies.

FOREWORD

For more than 50 years, the National Council on Economic Education (NCEE) has been calling attention to the need to educate our young people effectively in the skills of economics and personal finance and showing how that need can best be met. These new materials for teachers, sponsored by the Bank of America Foundation, provide an excellent and dramatic step in the direction of improving economic and financial literacy.

NCEE is proud of this splendid partnership with the Bank of America Foundation—and of the product.

We have found that students exposed to the economic way of thinking are more self-confident and more competent in making financial decisions, building their careers, and acting as informed citizens. By gaining understanding of the "real" world, we increase our prospects for better lives. Thanks to this distinctive program, we can now improve substantially on that kind of learning-for-life for millions of young people—who are our future.

NCEE's new multifaceted, comprehensive, and integrated program addresses the issue of economic and financial illiteracy by offering teaching-learning materials at four levels—grades K–2, 3–5, 6–8, and 9–12. There are 15 to 22 lessons in each part. Content for each of the grade levels is based on the *Voluntary National Content Standards for Economics*, which NCEE wrote and published, as well as the national guidelines for personal finance. Lessons are geared to active learning with games, simulations, role-playing, and computer use. All of the materials are also correlated with the extensive educational tools in personal finance and economics on our web site: **www.ncee.net**.

One exciting feature of these outstanding materials is that, for the first time, NCEE is offering parent guides for each educational level. Our research shows that students learn a considerable amount of their economic decision-making abilities from their parents. So NCEE is committed to assisting parents in the practical education of their children. These guidebooks are fun, as well as informative and instructive, for both students and their parents.

Nationally recognized experts in personal finance and economic education wrote the materials. Other experts and practitioners in the field reviewed them. The materials were then field-tested in three states over a period of two months. Each lesson was used by at least six teachers in urban, suburban, and rural settings. Refinements were made in the lessons according to the reviews from the field-testing.

We are proud of the results—which will now become the leading edge of personal finance education for all students, grades 6–8.

Our thanks go to many people for this important development. Without the visionary philanthropy of the Bank of America Foundation, this project would not have been possible. We are also indebted to the authors of each set of documents; their dedication, insight, and creativity will become immediately apparent to users of these materials in the classroom and at home. We are grateful as well to the reviewers of the materials, and to the teachers, parents, and students in California, Florida, and Texas who field-tested the materials. Finally, and especially, we thank

Dr. John E. Clow who directed the developmental work; because he has worked in the vineyard of economic and personal financial education for several decades, his knowledge of the field has been invaluable in orchestrating this significant project.

Robert F. Duvall, Ph.D.
President & Chief Executive Officer
The National Council on Economic Education (NCEE)

INTRODUCTION

The Financial Fitness for Life Curriculum consists of high-quality materials that assist students from kindergarten to grade 12 in making better decisions for earning income, spending, saving, borrowing, investing, and managing their money. The materials at the four levels (grades K–2, 3–5, 6–8, and 9–12) focus on a fitness theme.

Developing financial fitness is like developing physical fitness. Both require developing a knowledge base and then applying it. The development of knowledge for use in the everyday life of the students is a main goal of the lessons. Each level uses a fitness terminology. The headings for the different parts of each lesson include *Equipment* (materials needed), *Warm-up* (introduction to lesson), *Workout* (body of lesson), and *Cool Down* (summary and review). An analogous concept also stressed in the materials is that one must continually work on financial fitness, just as with physical fitness, because of new developments. The materials emphasize, though, that some basic routines are used consistently in order to maintain financial fitness, such as the importance of determining the cost of each choice and the realization that there is no free lunch.

Besides the fitness focus, some other features are common to all of the levels. They include:

1. Each set of materials is based on **national standards**. Matrices in this publication show how the materials relate to the national standards for economics and mathematics and the national guidelines for personal finance.

2. All materials employ economics, called **the science of decision making**, as a way to prioritize the staggering array of choices facing students when they make decisions. By prioritizing, students learn how to make better decisions, and, equally important, to avoid poor ones. The emphasis on using economic concepts and an economic way of thinking distinguishes these materials from other materials used to develop personal financial literacy. The economic concepts and economic ways of thinking are basic fitness routines used when a person deals with personal financial matters.

3. Active learning and student reflection on these activities dominate all materials. Active learning without reflection does not necessarily enhance true learning defined as changing behavior. Active learning *plus* reflection optimizes true learning. As with physical fitness, one must "do" and then "reflect" upon what one did in order to incorporate that learning into one's lifestyle.

4. Developing physical fitness involves doing a variety of exercises and varying those exercises over time. Similarly, these materials include a variety of methods that appeal to many different learning styles. Role playing, group discussions, gathering information from the Internet, reading materials, interviewing individuals, and analyzing case problems are some of the many teaching methods that are found in the materials. Even more materials are available on the web site of the National Council on Economic Education (**www.ncee.net**) to add to the repertoire of activities and materials.

5. A number of influential coaches can enhance the fitness process, especially when developing financial fitness. Parents as partners in the educational process are an integral part of this set

of materials. Parents play an important role in developing the personal financial literacy of their children because of the modeling that they do in everyday life. The lesson plans for each educational level have a parent guide, which provides background information and fun activities for both the parent and the child.

6. Similar to planning physical fitness activities for different ages, the economic and personal finance concepts are approached at the experiential/developmental level of the student. More abstract applications of economic and personal finance concepts are found at the higher educational levels than at the lower ones. The developmental approach to learning has been a hallmark of National Council on Economic Education (NCEE) materials for several decades.

Using the Teacher Guide for **Shaping Up Your Financial Future**

THE 17 LESSONS in the 6-8 document are divided into five theme areas: the economic way of thinking, earning an income, saving, spending and using credit, and managing money. Most of the lessons have several parts—taking two to three days to complete. Each lesson has a separate assessment component with evaluation activities ranging from paper-and-pencil quizzes to action-oriented tasks for students to do individually or in a group.

THE STUDENT WORKOUTS include reading materials about the content of the lessons plus worksheets to promote active, reflective learning. Each lesson has an introductory reading which is motivational as well as descriptive. The introduction includes the general focus of the lesson, vocabulary development, and the general concepts/ideas of the lesson.

THE PARENTS' GUIDE has activities that parents can do with their sons and daughters. The Guide includes content, worksheet activities, other activities, and resources. It is recommended that a guide be provided for each family. A letter to the parents from the teacher may help gain their cooperation. A reminder of when the parents should do a specific activity with a son or daughter would also help to encourage this school/home educational partnership. You may wish to have students report either orally or in writing on the activities they do with their parents.

Middle school students enjoy personal finance because it involves making decisions about their lives—both in the present and the future. Personal finance is an interdisciplinary area where language arts, computation skills, economics, finance, reasoning, and decision making are all brought together. We hope that you, your students, and their parents will enjoy the learning activities in these lessons and find them to be exciting, enriching experiences about some very important facts and skills for life.

John E. Clow, Ed.D.
Project Director
Financial Fitness for Life

Claire Melican
Vice President for Program Administration
National Council on Economic Education

TABLE 1

Correlation of **Shaping Up Your Financial Future** Lessons with Mathematics Standards and Benchmarks*

⬇Standards /Lessons➡	1	2	3	4	5	6	7	8	9	10	11	12	13	14	15	16	17
NUMBER AND OPERATION																	
Understand numbers, ways of representing numbers, relationships among numbers, and number systems.																	
• Work flexibly with fractions, decimals, and percents to solve problems.	✔		✔	✔				✔				✔					✔
• Develop meaning for percents greater than 100 and less than 1.											✔						
• Develop an understanding of large numbers and recognize and appropriately use exponential, scientific, and calculator notation.								✔									
• Use factors, multiples, prime factorization, and relatively prime numbers to solve problems.								✔				✔					
Understand meanings of operations and how they relate to one another.																	
• Understand the meaning and effects of arithmetic operations with fractions, decimals, and integers.	✔		✔	✔							✔	✔					
Compute fluently and make reasonable estimates.																	
• Select appropriate methods and tools for computing with fractions and decimals from among mental computation, estimation, calculators or computers, and paper and pencil, depending on the situation, and apply the selected methods.	✔		✔					✔									

TABLE 1 CONTINUED

⬇Standards /Lessons➡	1	2	3	4	5	6	7	8	9	10	11	12	13	14	15	16	17
• Develop and analyze algorithms for computing with fractions, decimals, and integers and develop fluency in their use.								✔									
MEASUREMENT STANDARD																	
Apply appropriate techniques, tools, and formulas to determine measurements.																	
• Solve problems involving scale factors, using ration and proportion.								✔				✔					
DATA ANALYSIS AND PROBABILITY STANDARD																	
Develop and evaluate inferences and predictions that are based on data.																	
• Use observations about differences between two or more samples to make conjectures about the populations from which the samples were taken.					✔												
PROBLEM SOLVING STANDARD																	
• Solve problems that arise in mathematics and in other contexts.						✔		✔			✔	✔			✔		
COMMUNICATION STANDARD																	
• Communicate their mathematical thinking coherently and clearly to peers, teachers, and others.	✔																
CONNECTIONS STANDARD																	
• Recognize and apply mathematics in contexts outside of mathematics.		✔	✔	✔			✔										
REPRESENTATION STANDARD																	
• Use representations to model and interpret physical, social, and mathematical phenomena.					✔												

* Standards taken from Principles and Standards for School Mathematics, *the National Council of Teachers of Mathematics (NCTM), 2000.*

TABLE 2

Correlation of **Shaping Up Your Financial Future** Lessons with the National Standards for Economics*

Lesson Number	1	2	3	4	5	6	7	8	9	10	11	12	13	14	15	16	17
Economic Standards																	
1. Scarcity	✔																
2. Marginal cost/marginal benefits		✔			✔	✔									✔	✔	
3. Role of incentives	✔										✔						
4. Markets—price and quantity determination			✔							✔							
5. Role of economic institutions								✔		✔						✔	
6. Role of interest rates							✔	✔		✔		✔					
7. Role of resources in determining income			✔	✔													
8. Profit and the entrepreneur			✔														
9. Role of government																	✔

* Taken from Voluntary National Content Standards in Economics, *National Council on Economic Education (NCEE), 1997.*

TABLE 3
Correlation of **Shaping Up Your Financial Future** Lessons with the National Personal Financial Management Guidelines*

Lesson Number	1	2	3	4	5	6	7	8	9	10	11	12	13	14	15	16	17
Personal Finance Management Guidelines																	
A. INCOME																	
1. Determinants of income			✔	✔	✔												
2. Sources of income				✔													✔
3. Taxes and transfer payments																	✔
B. MONEY MANAGEMENT																	
4. Opportunity Cost	✔				✔	✔	✔			✔	✔	✔			✔		
5. Short and long term financial goals						✔		✔	✔								
6. Budgeting						✔									✔		
7. Relationship between taxes, income, spending and financial investment																	✔
8. Risk management							✔		✔		✔						
9. Personal financial responsibility													✔	✔			
10. Perform basic financial operations						✔								✔			
C. SPENDING AND CREDIT																	
11. Spending now versus spending later												✔					
12. Costs and benefits of multiple transactions instruments												✔					
13. Risk and credit												✔					
14. Credit history and records													✔				
15. Rights and responsibilities of buyers, sellers, and creditors													✔				
16. Choosing among spending alternatives														✔			
17. Managing financial difficulties															✔		
D. SAVING AND INVESTING																	
18. Saving now versus saving later								✔									
19. Short and long term saving and investment strategies						✔											
20. Evaluate alternative investment decisions							✔		✔	✔							
21. Impact of government policies on saving and investment decisions							✔										

Taken from Personal Financial Management Guidelines and Benchmarks, *Jump$tart Coalition for Personal Financial Literacy, 1998.*

THEME 1

LESSON

1

The Economic Way of Thinking

Fitness Focus

EQUIPMENT AND GETTING READY!

Make overhead transparencies of the visuals listed here.

✔ Visual 1.1, *Limited Resources*
✔ Visual 1.2, *Every Choice Has An Opportunity Cost*
✔ Visual 1.3, *The Economic Way of Thinking*
✔ Visual 1.4, *Incentives Matter*
✔ Introductory reading for Theme 1 and Lesson 1 *(Shaping Up Your Financial Future Student Workouts)*
✔ Exercise 1.1, *Every Choice Has An Opportunity Cost (Shaping Up Your Financial Future Student Workouts)*
✔ Exercise 1.2 *Choosing the Better Incentive (Shaping Up Your Financial Future Student Workouts)*
✔ Exercise 1.3, *Using the Economic Way of Thinking (Shaping Up Your Financial Future Student Workouts)*
✔ Assessment 1.1, *The Economic Way of Thinking (Shaping Up Your Financial Future Student Workouts)*
✔ Family Activity 1, *Making Choices (The Parents' Guide to Shaping Up Your Financial Future)*
✔ Calculators
✔ One or two rolls of white adding machine paper (about 3 inches wide)
✔ Stopwatch

LESSON DESCRIPTION AND BACKGROUND

In this lesson, the students practice the *economic way of thinking*, a strategy for analyzing their own decisions as well as those of others. The *economic way of thinking* is based on the following principles:

▲ Resources are limited.
▲ People cannot have everything they want.
▲ People must make choices.
▲ Every choice involves a cost.
▲ People's choices have consequences.
▲ People respond to incentives.

The students engage in activities that require an analysis of choices, using the *economic way of thinking*.

This lesson is correlated with national standards for mathematics and economics as well as the national guidelines for personal financial management as shown in Tables 1 through 3 in the front of the book.

Student Objectives

At the end of this lesson, the student will be able to:

✔ Explain how limited resources necessitate choices.
✔ Identify the costs and benefits of a choice.
✔ Define opportunity cost.
✔ Identify and evaluate incentives.
✔ Analyze choices and predict consequences.

1

ECONOMIC AND PERSONAL FINANCE CONCEPTS

Opportunity cost, incentive, consequence

PARENT CONNECTION

Family Activity Worksheet l in *The Parents' Guide* focuses on having the parents and their son or daughter identify times when they had to make choices between alternatives involving a scarcity of time, space, or money. Identifying the opportunity cost and consequences of each choice is also a part of the activity. The role of incentives in choice making is also considered.

The Parents' Guide is a tool for reinforcing and extending the instruction provided in the classroom. It includes:

l. Content background in the form of frequently asked questions.

2. Interesting activities that parents can do with their son or daughter.

3. An annotated listing of books and Internet resources related to each theme.

Workout

WARM-UP

1. Introduce the idea of unlimited wants by giving each student a 3-foot strip of adding machine paper. Ask the students to list on the paper all the things they want that can be bought with money (this will eliminate the possibility of the students' listing intangibles, such as *world peace*).

2. At the end of three minutes, ask the students if they have listed everything they want. *(Most will probably say they have not.)*

3. Explain that human wants are unlimited. Even if the students had more than three minutes, they would probably not be able to list all their wants.

EXERCISE

1. Opportunity Cost

a. Using Visual 1.1, *Limited Resources*, explain that time, space, and money are limited, and people cannot have everything they want.

b. Have each student tape his or her list of wants to the board, and explain that it is the combination of unlimited human wants and limited resources that forces people to make economic choices.

c. Explain that every choice involves an *opportunity cost*—the next best alternative

that is given up when a choice is made. Display Visual 1.2, *Every Choice Has An Opportunity Cost*, and review the statements about how people have to make choices because of their unlimited wants and limited resources.

d. Discuss with the students the choices and opportunity costs in the three examples posed in Visual 1.2. *(When Sofia chooses to study, her opportunity cost is the time she could have used to read. When Maurice chooses to use his limited locker space for books, his opportunity cost is the* *space that could have been used for shoes. When Nguyen chooses to use his limited money to buy snacks, his opportunity cost is the movie ticket he could have bought.)*

e. Have the students suggest personal experiences that have involved limited time, space, or money. Have them identify their choices and opportunity costs. *(Students' discussion of personal experiences will vary, but they should focus on their choices and what they had to give up in each instance. They should use the term "opportunity cost" as they discuss their choices and what they gave up.)*

f. Divide the class into pairs, and have each pair complete Exercise 1.1, *Every Choice Has An Opportunity Cost*, in *Student Workouts*, following the examples given in Visual 1.2. When the students complete the exercise, engage them in a discussion of the statements they made. *(Sample answers: Shaundra can choose to get her mom a less expensive gift, or she can tell her mom she'll have the gift for her later, after she saves more money. If she chooses the less expensive gift, her opportunity cost is the necklace. Angelo's alternatives are to keep an aquarium or a stereo in his room. If he chooses the aquarium, his opportunity cost is the stereo. Raul's alternatives are to take the time to raise $15.00 or to spend the time doing something else. If Raul chooses to spend his time doing something else, his opportunity cost is to participate in the raffle.)*

2. Incentives

a. Have the students read the *Introduction* to Theme 1 and the *Warm-Up* and *Fitness Vocabulary* of Lesson 1 in *Student Workouts*. Discuss the new vocabulary, making sure the students understand the concepts.

b. Display Visual 1.3, *The Economic Way of Thinking*, and review the components with the class. Tell the students that by using the *economic way of thinking*, they will be better able to evaluate their own decisions and those of others.

c. Define *incentives* as factors that motivate and influence human behavior. Explain that incentives can be monetary (economic) or non-monetary (non-economic). *Monetary incentives* relate to money, income, and economic wealth. *Non-monetary incentives* motivate people for reasons other than money, wealth, or income. For example, parents might turn down higher-paying jobs in another town so that their children do not have to switch schools. Or a student might give up a baby-sitting job in order to spend time with friends.

d. Explain that in a market economy, pursuit of self-interest is an important motivator, whether that interest is monetary or non-monetary. For example, *entrepreneurs* take risks in order to start businesses in hopes of making lots of money. Non-monetary incentives can be physical, emotional, spiritual, or social. For example, people exercise to maintain good health and to look better. Those in religious orders provide care and shelter for the poor and sick because of a spiritual incentive to help others.

e. Display Visual 1.4, *Incentives Matter*. Have the students suggest responses to the "Choices" in the chart. *(Answers will vary; suggested responses are given on the next page.)*

f. Divide the class into pairs of students and distribute calculators. Have the students turn to Exercise 1.2, *Choosing the Better*

3

Choice	Economic Incentive	Non-Economic Incentive
Save half of baby-sitting money in a savings account.	Parents agree to match your savings, dollar for dollar.	You want to make a donation of money to AIDS victims. (Spiritual, emotional or social.)
Buy a new bike.	Price of bike is reduced.	You can get exercise riding the bike. (Physical.)
Open a charge account at a local store.	You can take advantage of sale prices.	There is prestige among peers to have a charge card. (Social.)
Lend $10 to a classmate.	Your friend will lend you money the next time you need it.	The classmate is a good friend. (Social.)
Join a walk-a-thon for charity.	Every participant gets a free T-shirt.	You feel good about yourself when you help others. (Spiritual or emotional.)

Incentive in *Student Workouts*. Have the students calculate the savings they would enjoy from each coupon, determine which is the better incentive in each instance, and record their decision and an explanation on the answer sheet. *(Answers are given below and on the next page.)*

g. Explain that when consumers are presented with different economic choices, they must be able to determine which one offers the greatest economic incentive.

3. Costs and Benefits

a. Ask the students to read *Muscle Developers* and *Showing Your Strength* in *Student Workouts*. Discuss their reactions to the two sections and answer any questions.

b. Explain that all choices involve *costs* and *benefits*. *Costs* are what you give up; *benefits* are what you gain when you make a choice.

c. Have the students work in small groups to complete Exercise 1.3, *Using the Economic Way of Thinking*, and discuss their answers. *[(1) Finances were limited; the students did not have enough money to pay for both a DJ and video show. (2) The committee chose the video-sound show. (3) Its incentive was the expectation of making more money. (4) The opportunity cost of choosing the video show was the choice of having the DJ. (5) Cost: higher priced entertainment carried risk of losing money. Benefit: possibility of making more money because more students would attend. (6) Consequences were that a larger number of students attended the dance, and the Honor Society made more money than expected. (7) No, the consequences do not always turn out as planned. With reasoned decisions, though, there is less chance for undesired consequences to occur.]*

1. Incentive #1 is the better deal.
#1: 20% off = $11.99 – $2.40 = $9.59
#2: Save $2.00 = $11.99 – $2.00 = $9.99

2. Incentive #2 is the better deal.
#1: Two boxes cost $5.18, get one free. Therefore, 3 boxes cost $5.18, or $1.73 each ($5.18 / 3).
#2: Save $1.00 on each box = $2.59 – $1.00 = $1.59 each.

3. Incentive #1 is the better deal.
#1: Two 32-oz jars cost $2.56, or $1.28 each, or $0.04 per ounce.
#2: Two 48-oz jars cost $5.98, minus $0.50 each = $4.98, divided by 96 ounces = $0.05 per ounce.

4. Incentive #2 is the better deal.
#1: $69.95 + $34.98 = $104.93 for two pairs.
#2: $100 for 2 pairs.

5. Incentive #2 is the better deal.
#1: $5 off = $240 ($40 x 6 tickets) + $7.99 for root beer = $247.99
#2: $45 x 5 tickets = $225

6. Incentive #1 is the better deal.
#1: 10% of $18 = $1.80 and $18.00 – $1.80 = $16.20
#2: $5.50 + $5.50 + $5.75 = $16.75

7. Both incentives are the same.
#1: 4 nights x $8.00 = $32.00; 2 nights x $4.00 = $8.00; $32 + $8 = $40.00
#2: 5 nights x $8.00 = $40.00; 1 night free; total = $40.00

8. Incentive #1 is the better deal.
#1: $16.99 + $16.99 = $33.98
#2: Two pizzas for $35.00

9. Incentive #2 is the better deal.
#1: $35.99 + $35.99 + $49.99 = $121.97 for three games.
#2: 3 games x $49.99 = $149.97 minus $29.99 (20%) = $119.98 for three games.

10. Incentive #2 is the better deal.
#1: $1.69 (4 oz bar) + $1.69 (4 oz bar) + free 2 oz. bar + $0.89 (2 oz bar) = $4.27 for 12 ounces.
#2: $0.69 x 6 two-oz. Bars = $4.14 for 12 ounces.

COOL DOWN

Have the students look through local newspapers to find articles about economic decisions. (Examples can be frivolous or serious, and can represent decisions in politics, entertainment, media, sports, business, etc.) Divide the class into groups and have each group analyze one decision using the *economic way of thinking.* Remind the students to examine choices, costs, benefits, incentives, and consequences. After the groups finish their analysis, engage the class in a discussion of each group's news articles and how the *economic way of thinking* helped them examine people's decisions.

Assessment

Students should complete Assessment 1.1. It asks them to identify the ideas presented in this lesson with real-life situations. The answer key is provided at the end of this lesson.

Other Training Equipment

An annotated bibliography and Internet resources can be found on our web site, **www.ncee.net**, and in *The Parents' Guide to Shaping Up Your Financial Future*.

Visual 1.1

Limited Resources

Because resources are limited, people can't have everything they want.

For example:

You can't go to a dance **and** to a basketball game on Friday night because **time** is limited.

You can't put a big screen TV **and** a pool table in the family room because **space** is limited.

You can't buy everything you see at the mall because **money** is limited.

Visual 1.2

Every Choice Has an Opportunity Cost

Because time, space, and money are limited, people can't have everything they want; they have to make choices. Every choice involves an opportunity cost—the next best alternative.

 **Because time is a limited resource, people have to make choices.**

Sofia must decide whether to finish her math assignment or read a book after dinner. If she chooses to use her time to do the math assignment, the opportunity cost is reading the book.

 **Because space is a limited resource, people have to make choices.**

Maurice must decide whether to put books or gym shoes on the shelf in his locker. If he chooses to use the shelf space for books, the opportunity cost is space for his shoes.

 **Because money is a limited resource, people have to make choices.**

Nguyen must decide whether to spend his allowance for snacks or a movie ticket. If he chooses to buy snacks, the opportunity cost is the movie ticket.

Visual 1.3

The Economic Way of Thinking

1 Resources are limited.

2 People cannot have everything they want.

3 People must make choices.

4 Every choice involves a cost.

5 People's choices have consequences.

6 People respond to incentives.

Financial Fitness for Life: Shaping Up Your Financial Future Teacher Guide, ©National Council on Economic Education

Visual 1.4

Incentives Matter

Choices	Economic Incentive	Non-Economic Incentive
Save half of earned baby-sitting money in a savings account.	Parents agree to match your savings, dollar for dollar.	
Buy a new bike.		You can get exercise riding the bike.
Open a charge account at a local store.		
Lend $10 to a classmate.		
Join a walk-a-thon for charity.		

What's the opportunity cost of each choice above?

ASSESSMENT

1.1 Answer Key

The Economic Way of Thinking

Distribute Assessment 1.1 (Shaping Up Your Financial Future Workouts) **and have each student complete it independently. Answers may vary. Some possible answers include:**

1. **Instead of putting an extra $3,000 in their retirement fund, Florence and Joe decided to fly from Chicago to Florida for a week of golf and relaxation.**

   ▲ Choice: *(Fly to Florida).*

   ▲ Opportunity cost: *(Add $3,000 to their retirement fund.)*

   ▲ Incentive: *(Chance to play golf and relax).*

   ▲ Consequence of their choice: *(Win a tournament; lose a golf club.)*

   ▲ Benefits: *(Meet new friends at the tournament; have a relaxing vacation.)*

2. **Brian and Sheryl paid their credit card debt instead of putting a down payment on a new convertible.**

   ▲ Choice: *(Paid credit card balance.)*

   ▲ Opportunity cost: *(Enjoyment of new convertible.)*

   ▲ Incentive: *(Eliminate monthly payments and high interest charges.)*

   ▲ Consequence of their choice: *(Had more money to save or spend on other purchases.)*

   ▲ How did Brian and Sheryl benefit from their choice? *(Had more disposable income to spend or save because they no longer had to pay monthly payments.)*

3. **Su-Zee, Lorena, and their friends went to the beach instead of working at the school book sale last weekend.**

   ▲ Choice: *(Weekend at the beach.)*

   ▲ Opportunity cost: *(Spending time with other friends at the book sale.)*

▲ Incentive: *(Get a suntan; enjoy a day at the beach.)*

▲ Consequence of their choice: *(Sunburn; friends at book sale angry that Su-Zee and friends didn't help at the book sale.)*

▲ How did Su-Zee, Lorena, and their friends benefit from their choice? *(Nice tan, day of fresh air and exercise, fun at the beach.)*

B. Using the economic way of thinking, **answer this question on the back of this sheet: Why do math teachers give homework every day?**

▲ Teacher's Choice: *(Give homework, have to check it.)*

▲ Opportunity Cost: *(Free time with no homework to check.)*

▲ Incentive for Making the Choice: *(Students will learn more; students will do better on tests).*

▲ Consequence of Choice: *(Missing good TV shows; less time with family.)*

▲ How/who benefits: *(Students learn more, do well and teacher gets good evaluations from parents, administrators; teacher has feeling of accomplishment.)*

Financial Fitness for Life: Shaping Up Your Financial Future Teacher Guide, ©National Council on Economic Education

THEME 1

LESSON

2

Consumer Decision Making

Fitness Focus

EQUIPMENT AND GETTING READY!

Make overhead transparencies of the visuals listed here.

✔ Visual 2.1, *The PACED Decision-Making Process*

✔ Visual 2.2, *Which Graham Cracker is Best?*

✔ Introductory reading for Lesson 2 (*Shaping Up Your Financial Future Student Workouts*)

✔ Exercise 2.1, *Which Graham Cracker Is Best?* (*Shaping Up Your Financial Future Student Workouts*)

✔ Exercise 2.2, *Using the PACED Decision-Making Process* (*Shaping Up Your Financial Future Student Workouts*)

✔ Exercise 2.3 (and PACED grid sheet), *Some Criteria are More Valuable Than Others* (*Shaping Up Your Financial Future Student Workouts*)

✔ Assessment 2.1, *Panel Discussion* (*Shaping Up Your Financial Future Student Workouts*)

✔ Family Activity 2, *How Can We Decide?* (*The Parents' Guide to Shaping Up Your Financial Future*)

✔ Product advertisements from newspapers or magazines

✔ 4" x 6" index cards (one per student)

✔ Construction paper and crayons or markers

✔ Three brands of graham crackers (or pretzels, soda crackers, etc.)

✔ Approximately 24 sandwich-sized plastic bags (Mark the bags "A," "B," and "C," and place 4–5 crackers of one brand in each bag. Be sure to note which brand is A, which is B, and which is C.)

✔ Paper cups (one per student) and water.

LESSON DESCRIPTION

In this lesson, the students learn that every decision involves alternatives. They practice using the PACED decision-making process:

▲ State the **P**roblem.

▲ List **A**lternatives.

▲ Identify **C**riteria.

▲ **E**valuate alternatives based upon criteria.

▲ Make a **D**ecision.

The PACED decision-making process is designed to help the students solve problems in a rational and systematic way. By recognizing what is important to them when they make a decision, the students will be able to evaluate their options and make more informed decisions.

This lesson is correlated with national standards for mathematics and economics as well as the national guidelines for personal financial management as shown in Tables 1 through 3 in the front of the book.

ECONOMIC AND PERSONAL FINANCE CONCEPTS

Opportunity cost, trade-off, alternatives, criteria, cost/benefit analysis

Student Objectives

At the end of this lesson, the student will be able to:

✔ Explain the purpose of a decision-making plan.

✔ Analyze a problem, using the PACED decision-making process.

✔ Explain why some criteria have more weight than others when using the decision-making process.

✔ Identify the costs and benefits of a decision.

PARENT CONNECTION

Family Activity 2 in *The Parents' Guide* involves having each student and his/her parent use the PACED decision-making process to make a family decision. Assign this family activity after you have covered the PACED process in class so that the students have familiarity with it. Have the students report on how they used the PACED process with their families.

The Parents' Guide is a tool for reinforcing and extending the instruction provided in the classroom. It includes:

1. Content background in the form of frequently asked questions.

2. Interesting activities that parents can do with their daughter or son.

3. An annotated listing of books and Internet resources related to each theme.

TIME REQUIRED 2 to 3 class periods

Workout

WARM-UP

1. Introduce the lesson by telling the students you've noticed that people often make impulsive decisions about what to buy. While this may not be a big problem when the product being purchased is a 59-cent candy bar, the situation can become critical if it is a $2,000 computer or a $30,000 car.

2. Have the students read the *Warm-Up* in Lesson 2 of *Student Workouts*, and stress that rational decision making is an important skill. Tell the students that if they begin to use sound decision-making strategies in minor situations, they will be ready to handle major decisions when they come along.

3. Tell the students that they will participate in a decision-making simulation. The purpose of the simulation is to demonstrate that good decisions are a result of recognizing options and evaluating costs and benefits.

4. Display Visual 2.1, *The PACED Decision-Making Process*, and review the five steps. Discuss the example on the visual, and ask the students to suggest other problems, alternatives, and criteria.

5. Emphasize that making a decision is the last step in the process and that decision making should always come after the process of recognizing alternatives, defining criteria, and evaluating the criteria.

EXERCISE

1. Which Graham Cracker Is Best?

a. Tell the students that they will use a decision-making process to select their favorite graham cracker. (Other items could be used, such as pretzels, vanilla wafers, or soda crackers.) After they identify their criteria, they will test several crackers to decide which one meets their definition of the best graham cracker.

b. Divide the class into groups of three or four students. Have the students turn to Exercise 2.1, *Which Graham Cracker is Best?* in *Student Workouts*. Display Visual 2.2. Instruct the students to list in the first row the characteristics they would look for when choosing a graham cracker. These characteristics are called *criteria*. (Answers will vary, but the students will probably mention taste, color, aroma, crunchiness, price, and nutritional content. If the students choose price as a criterion, tell them that you will tell them the price after the test. If they know before the test, price might influence their decision.)

c. Show the students the bags of graham crackers, and point out that there are three brands: A, B and C. These are the *alternatives*.

d. Distribute three bags of graham crackers (A, B and C) to each group and a small cup of water to each student.

e. Have the students taste the three different crackers. Instruct the students to "cleanse their palates" with some water between tasting each alternative. The one that best satisfies the taste criterion receives a score of 3, the next best one receives a 2, the least satisfactory cracker receives a 1. (This should be a group decision.)

f. Demonstrate how the grid in Visual 2.2 should be completed. Have the students continue to evaluate the crackers according to each of the other criteria, using the same "3-2-1" marking system.

g. When all groups have completed their evaluations, discuss the simulation with the class, emphasizing again the importance of identifying criteria before evaluating alternatives and making a decision.

h. After each group has expressed its preference and stated its reasons, reveal the

brands and the costs of each to the class and allow time for discussion and reactions. Show costs both as price per box and unit cost. Show the students how unit cost is figured by dividing the cost of the item by the weight. (Often the students are surprised to find out that a less expensive brand meets their criteria as well as, or better than, a costlier one.)

i. Explain that some decisions, such as choosing the best graham cracker, are all-or-nothing. (For example, if they were going to buy graham crackers, they would probably buy one brand and not another.) In an all-or-nothing situation, when they choose one alternative, they give up the chance to enjoy another one. The next best alternative they give up is the *opportunity cost*. (If Brand A is their favorite cracker, followed by Brand C and Brand B, then if they buy Brand A, Brand C is the opportunity cost—the next best alternative.)

j. Have the students read the *Fitness Vocabulary*, *Muscle Developers*, and *Showing Your Strength* in *Student Workouts*. Make sure the students understand the new vocabulary and concepts by engaging them in a discussion of the new terms.

2. Using the PACED Decision-Making Process

a. Have the students complete Exercise 2.2 in *Student Workouts* as an independent or small group assignment. *(Problem: At which store should I buy a new baseball mitt? Alternatives: Super-Star or Pro-Athlete Sporting Goods Stores. Criteria: price, selection, guarantee, time for shopping, exchange policy, location. Evaluate: Answers will vary. Accept any reasonable*

Criteria ▶ Alternatives ▼	Lower price	Wider selection	Better guarantee	More time to shop	Easier to return/exchange	Closer to home
Super-Star Sports Goods Store	Yes	No	No	No	No	Same
Pro-Athlete Sports Goods Store	No	Yes	Yes	Yes	Yes	Same

15

explanations. Decision: Answers will vary. Opportunity cost: If they buy a mitt at one store, buying a mitt at other store is the opportunity cost. A completed decision-making grid is shown on the preceding page.)

b. Explain that some choices, such as which baseball mitt to buy, are all-or-nothing. If you buy a mitt at one store, you won't buy a mitt at the other store. However, many times choices involve trade-offs, i.e., giving up a little of one thing in order to get a little more of something else. Point out that if the students have ever studied for one hour instead of two, they have traded off one hour of studying for one hour of watching television.

3. Some Criteria Are More Valuable Than Others

a. Explain that in some decision-making situations all the criteria are equally important (e.g., when choosing a graham cracker, taste and aroma may have the same value to you); however, in other decision-making situations, some criteria may be more important than others (e.g. when buying a new music CD, price is important, but it may not be as important as the type of music). Have the students suggest other examples. (When buying a new bike, price may be more important than color. When choosing a hair stylist, quality of work may be more important than price. When shopping for groceries, wide selection may be more important than location.)

b. Explain that when criteria have different degrees of importance, they can be given different values in the PACED grid.

c. Have the students read the opening paragraph of Exercise 2.3 in *Student Workouts*; point out how the values will be used to complete the grid, based upon the eight computer advertisements.

d. Have the students complete Exercise 2.3, using the grid in *Student Workouts* to record their answers. (Completed grid is shown below: Row D is highlighted; it is the choice.)

Criteria →		Less than $2000	17" monitor or larger	Stereo sound system	56K modem or faster	128 MB RAM or more	10 GB hard drive or more	Color printer	Total Value
Alternatives	**Value**	5	5	1	4	3	2	4	
A		0	5	1	0	3	2	4	15
B		5	5	1	0	0	0	4	15
C		5	0	0	4	3	0	4	16
D		5	5	1	4	0	2	4	21
E		5	0	1	0	3	2	0	11
F		5	0	1	4	3	2	4	19
G		0	5	1	4	3	2	4	19
H		5	5	0	4	0	2	4	20

Financial Fitness for Life: Shaping Up Your Financial Future Teacher Guide, ©National Council on Economic Education

e. Discuss the second question posed after the grid in Exercise 2.3. The students' explanation of why it would be best for the Noga family to buy Computer D should reflect a discussion of how the benefits of this particular product outweigh the costs of choosing some other one.

COOL DOWN

1. Display a number of advertisements from newspapers or magazines, pointing out the criteria noted in each ad (e.g., an ad for a sports drink might mention taste, vitamin content, price, quick thirst-quenching, etc.). Ask each student to list on a 4" × 6" index card, a good or service s/he has purchased in the past month. The students should also list the criteria that they value in that product.

2. Have the students exchange cards and use construction paper and markers to design an advertisement for the product on their cards, making sure to highlight and illustrate the criteria. (For example, if the item is a CD player, they should highlight criteria such as size, price, sound quality, number of functions, and portability.)

Assessment

Distribute Assessment 2.1 in *Student Workouts* and allow enough time for the students to conduct research and prepare their panel discussions. (Responses will vary; assess each group/individual based upon the following: facts presented; relevance of facts to demographics of Group A, B, or C; appropriate use of the PACED decision-making process; clear, concise communication of information.)

Other Training Equipment

An annotated bibliography and additional Internet resources are available on our web site, **www.ncee.net**, and in *The Parents' Guide* to *Shaping Up Your Financial Future.*

Visual 2.1

The PACED Decision-Making Process

P State the **problem.**

A List the **alternatives.**

C Identify the **criteria.**

E **Evaluate** the alternatives based upon the criteria.

D Make a **decision.**

Problem: I don't have enough time to finish two big assignments.

Alternatives: I can do my math homework or finish my science project.

Criteria: I have an A average in math and a C average in science. The math assignment is worth 10% of my math grade; the science project is worth 25% of my science grade. I've missed two assignments in math; I haven't missed any assignments in science.

Evaluate: Because I'm not doing so well in science, and the science project is worth more, it's more important for me to finish the science project (even though I have a missing math assignment).

Decision: I'll finish the science project.

Visual 2.2

Which Graham Cracker Is Best?

Alternatives \ Criteria →					
A					
B					
C					

THEME 2

LESSON

3

Career Choice Making

Fitness Focus

Make overhead transparencies of the visuals listed here.

✔ Visual 3.1, *What Is Human Capital?*

✔ Visual 3.2, *Human Capital Score Sheet*

✔ Visual 3.3, *Answers to Demand for Labor in Various Occupational Areas*

✔ Visual 3.4, *SCANS Skills*

✔ Visual 3.5, *The Role of the Entrepreneur in the Economy*

✔ Activity 3.1A and B, *Success Depends on Human Capital*, Group A & B

✔ Activity 3.2A and B, *Success Depends on Human Capital*, Group A & B *(optional)*

✔ Introductory reading for Theme 2 and Lesson 3 *(Shaping Up Your Financial Future Student Workouts)*

✔ Exercise 3.1, *Demand for Labor in Various Occupational Areas (Shaping Up Your Financial Future Student Workouts)*

✔ Exercise 3.2, *Self-Assessment (Shaping Up Your Financial Future Student Workouts)*

✔ Exercise 3.3, *Human Capital and SCANS on the Job (Shaping Up Your Financial Future Student Workouts)*

✔ Exercise 3.4, *How Do Entrepreneurs Earn a Living? (Shaping Up Your Financial Future Student Workouts)*

✔ Assessment 3.1, *What's Wrong With This Picture? (Shaping Up Your Financial Future Student Workouts)*

✔ Family Activity 3, *What Career Interests You? (The Parents' Guide to Shaping Up Your Financial Future)*

✔ Stopwatch

✔ Calculators

LESSON DESCRIPTION

In this lesson, the students learn that career choices are easier to make if they understand the job market, recognize their own aptitudes, and realize the relationship between marketable skills and workplace success. They will begin by examining statistics projecting the future demand for various occupations. Then they will complete a self-assessment to identify career pathways that match their interests and abilities. After evaluating a number of job descriptions, they will compare each job's requirements to the skills recommended by SCANS (Secretary's Commission on Achieving Necessary Skills). Finally, the students will consider entrepreneurship as a career option, defining the characteristics of successful entrepreneurs.

This lesson is correlated with national standards for mathematics and economics as well as the national guidelines for personal financial management as shown in Tables 1 through 3 in the front of the book.

Student Objectives

At the end of this lesson, the student will be able to:

✔ Examine projected demand for a variety of occupations in relation to one's interests.

✔ Analyze how human capital is related to career choices and opportunities.

✔ Recognize the importance of investment in human capital.

✔ Explain the relationship of worker productivity to education and experience.

✔ Describe the characteristics of an entrepreneur.

✔ Explain how entrepreneurs benefit the economy.

ECONOMIC AND PERSONAL FINANCE CONCEPTS

Human capital, entrepreneur, opportunity cost

PARENT CONNECTION

Family Activity 3 in *The Parents' Guide* involves having the student work with his/her parents in using the PACED decision-making process for making some career/job choices. A career interest self-assessment is also a part of the parent guide activity for this lesson. You may want the students to write a short paper on what they learned from doing the activities with their parents.

The Parents' Guide is a tool for reinforcing and extending the instruction provided in the classroom. It includes:

1. Content background in the form of frequently asked questions.
2. Interesting activities that parents can do with their son or daughter.
3. An annotated listing of books and Internet resources related to each theme.

TIME REQUIRED 3 to 4 class periods

Workout

WARM-UP

1. Ask what skills, knowledge, and experience the cook in the school cafeteria must have. *(Knowledge of sanitation, reading and math skills to follow recipes and calculate measurements, and knowledge or experience using kitchen equipment, etc.)* Tell the students these abilities or skills are called the cook's *human capital.*

2. Display Visual 3.1, *What Is Human Capital?* and have the students suggest responses for the listed occupations. *(Answers will vary; suggested answers are given below.)*

Pilot	Marine Biologist	Web Designer	TV Reporter
Good vision and eye-hand coordination; knowledge of plane operation; understanding of weather patterns and air pressure; confidence.	Unafraid of water; education in biology and oceanography; apprenticeship in marine biology program; patience.	Keyboarding, installing software; education in information technology; internship at a software company; creativity.	Pleasant voice; good reader; understanding and interest in geography, world events; college TV station or radio station experience; articulate.

EXERCISE

1. Insiders and Outsiders.

  a. Demonstrate how knowledge can improve human capital by having the students complete the following simulation.

  b. Divide the class into two teams: Group A and Group B.

  c. Distribute Activity 3.1A *Success Depends Upon Human Capital Group A,* **face down,** to Group A, and Activity 3.1B *Success Depends Upon Human Capital Group B,* **face down,** to Group B.

21

d. Explain to the students that they will participate in a timed exercise. They are not to begin until told to do so. When they complete the exercise, they should raise their hands, and you will call out their times. They should write their own time at the bottom of the sheet.

e. Explain that if some students have not completed the exercise at the end of five minutes, time will be called. Those students will receive a maximum score of five minutes.

f. Students who finish in fewer than five minutes should sit quietly and not disturb others who are attempting to complete the exercise.

g. Instruct only the *Group A* students to turn over their papers and read the directions at the top.

h. When all the *Group A* students have read the directions, start the stopwatch and have the *Group B* students turn their papers over and both groups begin the exercise.

i. Call out the elapsed times for the students as they raise their hands signaling that they have completed the exercise.

j. At the end of five minutes, call "time," and instruct the students who have not completed the exercise to write "5 minutes" on their sheets.

k. Provide the answers but **do not** reveal the secret of the code: *(1) The rock concert last Saturday was really great. (2) My uncle bought a new red sports car. (3) Every person in my family has a ton of freckles. (4) I enjoy playing video games with my friends. (5) During the game our coach became angry with the umpire.*

l. Display Visual 3.2, *Human Capital Score Sheet*. Ask the *Group A* students to raise their hands if their time was between zero and one minute. Record in the first cell of the grid the number of students whose hands are raised. Continue to count the students and record numbers until the top

portion of the chart is complete for both *Group A* students and *Group B* students.

OPTIONAL: To demonstrate how experience can also improve human capital:

▲ Distribute Activity 3.2A face down to the *Group A* students and Activity 3.2B face down to the *Group B* students. Start the clock, and have both groups read the directions and repeat the Exercise.

▲ Provide the answers: *(1) When my mom bakes bread, the whole house smells delicious. (2) At the park near my house there is a new soccer field. (3) Our garage is cluttered with old bikes and lawn mowers. (4) At the eighth grade dance our principal wore a black tuxedo. (5) In science we learned how to separate hydrogen and oxygen.*

▲ Display Visual 3.2 again and complete the bottom portion, once again having the students comment on the results. *(Times may be more similar in this round, although Insiders may still perform more quickly because of their previous experience.)*

m. Engage the students in a discussion of the differences in the scores of the two groups. Pose the questions on the bottom of Visual 3.2. *(Group A students were faster [more productive] because of **knowledge** of the code. Knowledge increases productivity. **Experience** [second round] also usually increases the speed with which students solve the puzzles. So, experience increases productivity. Employers look for people with schooling [knowledge], experience, and a willingness to learn.)*

2. Have the students read the *Introduction* to Theme 2 and the *Warm-Up, Fitness Vocabulary, Muscle Developers*, and *Showing Your Strength* of Lesson 3 in *Student Workouts*. Discuss the new terms, making sure the students understand the new terminology.

3. Demand for Labor in Various Occupations

a. Explain that choosing the right career should be based upon a person's interests and abilities and upon the demand for certain occupations. For example, because the demand for workers who make and repair watches is very low, it would probably not be a good idea for the students to invest time and effort learning to make or repair watches. However, they would be wise to acquire skills, knowledge, and experience in fields of interest that are in high demand: computer technology, health care, engineering, etc.

b. Have the students look at Exercise 3.1, *Demand for Labor in Various Occupational Areas* in *Student Workouts*, and discuss the data with the class. Ask the students to suggest reasons for the projected growth or decline in the demand for various fields of work. *(Answers will vary, but the students should observe that occupations in technology and services are expected to be more abundant than occupations in manufacturing and agriculture. In the United States, demand for occupations that require more mental than physical labor seems to be growing.)*

c. Explain that knowing which occupational areas are expected to grow can help the students plan the direction to take in their own career preparation. Aiming toward high-demand occupations can provide more opportunities when the time comes to enter the world of work, and investing in their human capital through education and training can make students more marketable in the workplace.

d. Remind the students that they should also consider their own interests, aptitudes and goals when making career choices. For example, even though the demand for agricultural workers may not be growing, people with certain kinds of human capital and interests are needed to replace those who leave the job or retire.

e. Divide the class into groups of four or five students and have them work together to calculate the percent of projected increase or decrease in the occupational areas listed in Exercise 3.1. Students who are familiar with the use of spreadsheets might wish to use a computer to perform the calculations and then create graphs depicting the results. *(Answers shown in Visual 3.3.)*

f. Have each student create a small poster depicting the change in one of the 32 interest areas. The poster should include a graph and a short paragraph expressing the student's interpretation of the data.

g. Review with students the ideas that investing in human capital and being aware of the demand for certain occupations are the first steps toward making career choices. The next step is an assessment of their own likes and dislikes.

4. Occupational Self-Assessment

a. Have students complete Exercise 3.2, *Self-Assessment*, as an independent assignment. After they have analyzed their aptitudes for several career clusters, engage the class in a discussion of the results of their surveys.

b. Remind the students that choosing a career—just like any other choice—involves an opportunity cost. For example, if a student chooses to be a doctor, she or he must give up the opportunity to be a forest ranger at the same time.

23

c. Explain that every job requires skills. Display Visual 3.4, *Scans Skills,* and discuss.

d. Point out that most employers spell out the requirements necessary for success in their companies.

e. Have the students read one or two classified ads in Exercise 3.3 and discuss the skills required.

f. Have the students work independently to complete Exercise 3.3, *Human Capital and SCANS on the Job. (Answers will vary. Accept any response that the students can logically defend. Suggested answers are given below. The letters the students write should adequately describe how their human capital satisfies the job requirements.)*

5. The Role of the Entrepreneur

a. Explain that choosing a career often means working for a small company or a big corporation, but it can also mean working for yourself. Define *entrepreneur* as an innovator who takes a risk to create a business in order to earn a profit. Explain that entrepreneurs provide goods and services that add variety and choice to the marketplace. Entrepreneurs also provide jobs.

b. Display Visual 3.5, *The Role of the Entrepreneur in the Economy*, and discuss.

c. Explain that entrepreneurs are risk-takers. When they choose to work for themselves, their opportunity cost is the security of a guaranteed paycheck every week.

d. Have the students work in pairs to complete Exercise 3.4, *How Do Entrepreneurs Earn a Living? (Answers: A. Dimitrio would earn $3,360 a month at his old job, which would have included his insurance and retirement. His expenses in his new business were $26,465 in July; therefore he must have earned $29,825 in July to pay his expenses and pay himself $3,360. [$3360 + 26,465 = $29,825] B. Answers will vary. If Dimitrio was tired of working for someone else, running his own business and being his own boss may be best for him. However, when an entrepreneur assumes greater risk [of failing, not earning a profit], a greater gain should be the reward. Dimitrio is not getting a greater monetary return for assuming more risk, so perhaps it is not worth the risk. BONUS: Dimitrio's salary was 11.3% of his July revenues. [$3,360 ÷ 29,835 = .1126 × 100 = 11.3%.])*

Answers to Exercise 3.3

SCANS Skills	Ad Number	SCANS Skills	Ad Number
Basic Skills	1, 7, 8	Problem Solving	5, 7, 9, 10
Interpersonal Skills	1, 4, 6	Good Work Ethic	2, 10
Teamwork	2, 3, 4, 7	Experience	2, 5, 6, 8
Use Technology	1, 4, 5, 7, 8, 9, 10	Organizational Skills	2, 4, 6, 9
Communication	1, 3, 7, 9, 10		

COOL DOWN

1. Review the following questions with the students:

a. What is human capital? *(Human capital includes the intellect, knowledge, experience, skills, and attitudes that a person possesses or learns.)*

b. What are some ways to develop your human capital? *(Education and work experience develop human capital.)*

c. Why should you look at the demand for an occupation when you consider making a career choice? *(To determine whether jobs will be available after you have prepared for that career.)*

d. What other things besides demand for an occupation should you consider when making a career choice? *(The occupations most interesting to you, and the occupations in which you have an aptitude.)*

e. What are some major differences between being an employee and being an entrepreneur? *(An employee works for someone else and does what the employer wants him or her to do. An entrepreneur chooses his or her work and may hire others to work in the business. Employees receive wages or salaries for their work; entrepreneurs take a risk and earn income from profits [or lose money].)*

Assessment

Students should complete Assessment 3.1 in *Student Workouts* as a homework assignment. When the assignment is complete, have the students review in class the SCANS skills that Kelly did not exhibit. The answer key is provided at the end of this lesson.

Other Training Equipment

An annotated bibliography and Internet resources are available on our web site, **www.ncee.net**, as well as in *The Parents' Guide to Shaping Up Your Financial Future*.

Visual 3.1

What Is Human Capital?

Human capital includes the intellect, knowledge, experience, and attitude necessary for success.

Human Capital Needed for These Occupations:

Pilot	Marine Biologist	Web Designer	TV Reporter

Financial Fitness for Life: Shaping Up Your Financial Future Teacher Guide, ©National Council on Economic Education

Visual 3.2

Human Capital Score Sheet

		GROUP A	GROUP B
Round 1	0:00 – 1:00 Minute		
	1:01 – 2:00 Minutes		
	2:01 – 3:00 Minutes		
	3:01 – 4:00 Minutes		
	4:01 – 5:00 Minutes		
	5:00 Max Minutes		
Optional Round 2	0:00 – 1:00 Minute		
	1:01 – 2:00 Minutes		
	2:01 – 3:00 Minutes		
	3:01 – 4:00 Minutes		
	4:01 – 5:00 Minutes		
	5:00 Max Minutes		

▲ Who solved the codes faster? Why?

▲ What can you say about the effect of information and knowledge on human capital?

▲ If you completed Round 2, what can you say about the effect of experience on human capital?

Visual 3.3

Answers to Demand for Labor in Various Occupational Areas

A INDUSTRY	B Actual Number Employed in 1998	C Projected Number Employed in 2008	D Change in Number from 1998–2008 (Col C – Column B) Indicate + or −	E Percentage Change 1998–2008 (Col D / Column B) Indicate + or −
Education	11,174,900	12,884,700	1,709,800	15.3%
Hospitals	4,909,200	5,284,900	375,700	7.7%
Savings institutions	1,904,900	1,932,000	27,100	1.4%
Federal government	1,819,100	1,654,600	−164,500	−9.0%
Nursing facilities	1,762,000	2,212,900	450,900	25.6%
Computer services	1,599,300	3,471,300	1,872,000	117.1%
Agriculture, forestry, fishing	1,154,000	1,006,200	−147,800	−12.8%
Legal services	972,500	1,200,000	227,500	23.4%
Engineering	905,200	1,140,000	234,800	25.9%
Residential care	745,700	1,171,000	425,300	57.0%
Child care	604,500	800,000	195,500	32.3%
Apparel manufacturing	547,100	650,000	102,900	18.8%
TV, radio, music stores	500,300	639,800	139,500	27.9%
Newspapers	442,500	401,000	−41,500	−9.4%
Beauty salons	410,500	465,000	54,500	13.3%
Non-store retailers	346,400	537,200	190,800	55.1%
Medical supplies	279,100	334,600	55,500	19.9%
Advertising	268,200	323,200	55,000	20.5%
Radio & TV broadcasting	246,900	253,000	6,100	2.5%
Railroad transportation	230,700	184,900	−45,800	−19.9%
Retail bakeries	206,400	247,700	41,300	20.0%
Personal credit	185,200	246,600	61,400	33.2%
Cable and pay TV	181,000	230,000	49,000	27.1%
Video tape rental	165,300	184,900	19,600	11.9%
Knitting mills	159,400	127,800	−31,600	−19.8%
Motion picture theaters	138,100	135,200	−2,900	−2.1%
Commercial sports	126,500	160,000	33,500	26.5%
Funeral services	99,400	110,100	10,700	10.8%
Museums and zoos	92,600	131,400	38,800	41.9%
Coal mining	91,600	59,400	−32,200	−35.2%
Luggage and leather	45,400	34,400	−11,000	−24.2%
Tobacco products	40,600	29,500	−11,100	−27.3%

Visual 3.4

SCANS Skills

The Secretary's Commission on Achieving Necessary Skills (SCANS) report from the United States Department of Labor, presented a national model of skills that every worker needs in order to be productive and successful.

The SCANS skills include:

BASIC SKILLS:

▲ Reading, writing, math, listening

OTHER SKILLS:

▲ Interpersonal skills

▲ Team work

▲ Use of technology and other resources

▲ Communication (both oral and written)

▲ Problem solving

▲ Organizational skills

▲ Positive attitude/good work ethic

SCANS Competencies describe a person's **human capital—** a combination of intellect, knowledge, experience, and attitude.

Financial Fitness for Life: Shaping Up Your Financial Future Teacher Guide, ©National Council on Economic Education

Visual 3.5

The Role of the Entrepreneur in the Economy

Entrepreneurs are innovators

They observe an opportunity.

They create new goods and services.

They improve existing products.

Entrepreneurs provide choice

They add goods and services to the marketplace.

They offer variety.

They design different approaches to familiar problems.

Entrepreneurs provide jobs

They hire workers for their businesses.

They consume resources, thus providing jobs in the industries that supply those resources.

Entrepreneurs help the economy grow.

Financial Fitness for Life: Shaping Up Your Financial Future Teacher Guide, ©National Council on Economic Education

ACTIVITY 3.1A

Success Depends Upon Human Capital (Group A)

Each sentence below is written in code. **CLUE:** The last word in the mixed-up sentence is the first word in the real sentence. The first word in the mixed-up sentence is the second word in the real sentence. (Example: if the mixed-up sentence is **Prefer butter instead candy of cookies peanut I**. The real sentence would be **I prefer peanut butter cookies instead of candy**. The words are numbered below to show you how it works.)

2	4	6	8	7	5	3	1
Prefer	butter	instead	candy	of	cookies	peanut	I

Rewrite the deciphered message below each coded one. Raise your hand when you are finished, and when your teacher calls out your time, write it in the blank at the bottom of the page.

Rock last was great really Saturday concert the.

Uncle a red car sports new bought my.

Person my has ton freckles of a family in every.

Enjoy video with friends my games playing I.

The our became with umpire the angry coach game during.

MY TIME _____

31

Success Depends Upon Human Capital (Group B)

Each sentence below is written in code. Rewrite the deciphered message below each coded one. Raise your hand when you are finished, and when your teacher calls out your time, write it in the blank at the bottom of the page.

Rock last was great really Saturday concert the.

Uncle a red car sports new bought my.

Person my has ton freckles of a family in every.

Enjoy video with friends my games playing I.

The our became with umpire the angry coach game during.

MY TIME _____

Success Depends Upon Human Capital (Group A)

Each sentence below is written in code. **CLUE: The last word in the mixed-up sentence is the first word in the real sentence. The first word in the mixed-up sentence is the second word in the real sentence.** (Example: if the mixed-up sentence is **Prefer butter instead candy of cookies peanut I.** The real sentence would be **I prefer peanut butter cookies instead of candy.** The words are numbered below to show you how it works.)

2	4	6	8	7	5	3	1
Prefer	butter	instead	candy	of	cookies	peanut	I

Rewrite the deciphered message below each coded one. Raise your hand when you are finished, and when your teacher calls out your time, write it in the blank at the bottom of the page.

My bakes the house delicious smells whole bread mom when.

The near house is new field soccer a there my park at.

Garage cluttered old and mowers lawn bikes with is our.

The grade our wore tuxedo a principal dance eighth at.

Science learned to hydrogen oxygen and separate how we in.

MY TIME _____

Financial Fitness for Life: Shaping Up Your Financial Future Teacher Guide, ©National Council on Economic Education

Success Depends Upon Human Capital (Group B)

Each sentence below is written in code. Rewrite the deciphered message below each coded one. Raise your hand when you are finished, and when your teacher calls out your time, write it in the blank at the bottom of the page.

My bakes the house delicious smells whole bread mom when.

The near house is new field soccer a there my park at.

Garage cluttered old and mowers lawn bikes with is our.

The grade our wore tuxedo a principal dance eighth at.

Science learned to hydrogen oxygen and separate how we in.

MY TIME _____

ASSESSMENT

3.1 Answer Key

What's Wrong With This Picture?

Have the students complete Assessment 3.1 as an independent assignment. (Answers are given below in bold.)

Kelly is a seventh grader at Middleville Middle School. Her first class begins at 8:05, so she sets her alarm for 7:30. That way she's out of the kitchen door at 7:50 and **ready for her 20-minute walk to school. (G)** Yesterday, when she entered the building, she saw the principal, Ms. Ramirez.

"Yo," (E) Kelly shouted. "What's happenin'?"

"You're late, Kelly," said the principal, frowning.

"Whatever!" (E) replied Kelly, as she raced down the hall.

In class, Kelly ruffled through her book bag but **could not find any pens, pencils, or paper. (H)** When Mr. Choy asked for her math assignment, she didn't have that either.

"You'll have to go to the office," Mr. Choy told her.

In the principal's office, Kelly was asked to answer the phone while one of the secretaries stepped out. When the phone rang, Kelly picked it up.

"Hey, man, this is Middleville school. Whaddya want?" (E) she said.

The caller hung up, but Kelly could not figure out why. She decided to leave a note for the secretary. It said: **"Deer Sekretery, Somebody called and hung up. I dont no who it was." (A)**

When the phone rang again, Kelly said, **"Whooze zis?" (E)**

"Please have Ms. Ramirez call the superintendent's office by 9:30."

"Okay, okay," said Kelly. On a piece of scrap paper she wrote: "Ms. Ramirez—**go to the custodian's office after 9:30." (A)**

"Kelly, you need to keep a good record of the calls," said the school clerk.

"You can't tell me what to do," shouted Kelly. **"I'm doin' ya a favor by helpin' ya out." (B)**

The next day when Kelly woke up, it was dark in her bedroom. She flipped the switch about ten times, but her lamp would not light.

"Hey, what's wrong with my lamp?" she yelled to her mother.

"Maybe the bulb burned out," her mother suggested.

"Oh, I never thought of that," **(F)** said Kelly.

Kelly was upset, so she decided not to go to school. **"Let's see, that's 15 days absent so far this year. That ain't too bad." (G)**

When Kelly returned to school her social studies teacher, Ms. Musielewicz, sent her to the computer lab to do some research for a big project. In the lab, Kelly was clueless. **She did not even know how to turn on the computer. (D)** The lab assistant tried to help her, but Kelly just shrugged.

"I took that stupid computer class last year, but I didn't like it. Besides, I'm gonna be a mechanic when I'm done with school. **I don't need no computer skills." (E)**

Finally, it was the last period of the day—gym class. The substitute teacher was assigning the students to teams for basketball. When Kelly got the ball, she dribbled down the floor and tried to shoot, even though she was surrounded by players from the other team.

"Pass. Pass the ball!" shouted the teacher.

But Kelly just tried to shoot again and was blocked by another player. Every time she got the ball, Kelly tried to shoot. **She never passed to another player. (C)**

When the bell rang at the end of the day, Kelly grabbed her book bag and ran out of the building. On the way home she stopped at the store and bought a candy bar for $0.55, giving the clerk a one-dollar bill.

"With tax, that's 59 cents. Your change is 31 cents," the cashier said, handing Kelly a quarter, a nickel and a penny.

"Hey," said another shopper. "That's not the right change."

"Sure it is," shrugged Kelly. **"It must be. The man said it was." (A)**

When Kelly got home, her mother asked how things went at school.

"All right, I guess," she replied. "But I can't wait to finish and get a job. Then I can do anything I want."

Responses to the last section: the advice to Kelly will vary. The students should list ways for Kelly to improve her SCANS skills through education, experiences, and investment in her own human capital.

THEME 2

LESSON

4

Productivity

Fitness Focus

EQUIPMENT AND GETTING READY!

Make overhead transparencies of the visuals listed here.

✔ Visual 4.1, *The Story of Mike and Chris, Inc.*

✔ Visual 4.2, *Increasing Productivity of Workers*

✔ Visual 4.3, *Checks*

✔ Introductory reading for Lesson 4 *(Shaping Up Your Financial Future Student Workouts)*

✔ Exercise 4.1, *The Whole Story (Shaping Up Your Financial Future Student Workouts)*

✔ Assessment 4.1, *Career Search (Shaping Up Your Financial Future Student Workouts)*

✔ Family Activity 4, *What Do You Really Do At Work? (The Parents' Guide to Shaping Up Your Financial Future)*

✔ Calculators

LESSON DESCRIPTION

In this lesson, the students examine ways to develop their human capital, that is, their value as a human resource. They discover that by developing their human capital, they make themselves more productive. They also find that they can be more productive by using capital resources, the tools of their trade. The more productive they become as a human resource, the more valuable they will become to their employer. Ultimately, they find that the more valuable they are to their employer, the greater their income will usually be. With greater income, the consumer can have a higher standard of living.

This lesson is correlated with national standards for mathematics and economics as well as the national guidelines for personal financial management as shown in Tables 1 through 3 in the front of the book.

ECONOMIC AND PERSONAL FINANCE CONCEPTS

Capital resources, human capital, wage, productivity

Student Objectives

At the end of this lesson, the student will be able to:

✔ Give examples of capital resources used in various careers.

✔ Explain in what ways the use of capital resources increases productivity.

✔ Explain ways in which productivity can be increased.

✔ State the human capital required for particular jobs.

✔ Explain how those skills are acquired.

PARENT CONNECTION

Family Activity 4 in *The Parents' Guide* is an interview form that a student should use to interview one or both parents about the job each holds. You may want students to synthesize the findings of their interview in a written paper.

The Parents' Guide is a tool for reinforcing and extending the instruction provided in the classroom. It includes:

1. Content background in the form of frequently asked questions.
2. Interesting activities that parents can do with their son or daughter.
3. An annotated listing of books and Internet resources related to each theme.

TIME REQUIRED 1 to 2 class periods

Workout

WARM-UP

1. Introduce the lesson by asking the students what workers receive in return for their work. The returns might include self-gratification and self-esteem. The economic return to labor is wages and benefits. Display Visual 4.1, *The Story of Mike and Chris, Inc.*, and explain that some workers are more valuable to an employer than others.

2. Point out that Yolanda considered Mike to be more productive than Chris because Mike could accomplish more work than Chris in the same amount of time while using the same amount of resources. Workers can increase their productivity in a variety of ways.

EXERCISE

1. Increasing Productivity

a. Display Visual 4.2, *Increasing Productivity of Workers*, and explain that employees can use capital resources to increase their productivity. *Capital resources* are goods produced for the purpose of producing other goods and services. For instance, a hammer is a capital resource. A hammer is produced to aid in construction.

b. Explain that developing human capital can also increase productivity. *Human capital* is the combination of education, skills, and talents a worker gathers over time. The development of human capital enhances your value as a worker. Imagine that on the day you were born, you were given a large, empty box. Now imagine that as you completed each grade level, you were able to place all of the skills you acquired in the box.

c. Ask the students what types of skills they would have in their box at this time in their lives. *(Reading skills, math skills, social skills, critical thinking skills, and athletic skills.)* Explain that they will acquire many other skills by the time they are looking for their first full-time jobs. At that time, they will present their skill set to their employers as if they were offering their employers a gift box of skills that the employers could use to build their businesses.

d. Explain that the quality of workers' human capital will likely determine their level of income. In general, the better-educated people are, and the more skills they acquire, the more valuable those employees are. The employer will compensate workers according to the skills they bring to their jobs.

e. Remind the students that their human capital contributes to their productivity. Ask them to recall that Mike was more productive at cutting grass than Chris was. Ask the students to imagine a situation where Mike and Chris are not in business together, but rather competing for the same $8.00 per hour grass-cutting job. Which of the boys would get the job? *(Mike would be more likely to be hired when productivity in grass cutting is the determining factor.)*

f. Explain that when people acquire higher levels of education or practice their skills, they are investing in their human capital. They are investing in themselves.

g. Direct the students to Exercise 4.1, *The Whole Story*, and explain that they are going to read more about Mike and Chris's grass-cutting service.

h. Discuss the questions in Exercise 4.1. The students might suggest that Chris was not as tall or strong as Mike, or that he was lazy. However, Chris had a different skill set that allowed him to be a productive worker. Even though Mike cut the grass more quickly, it was Chris who had the social and business skills that allowed him to approach customers and sell the service. Summarize the discussion by explaining that people have different physical and personal qualities that can make them better suited for some jobs than for others.

i. Have the students read the *Warm-Up*, *Fitness Vocabulary*, *Muscle Developers*, and *Showing Your Strength* of Lesson 4 in *Student Workouts*. Ask questions of the students to determine their understanding of the concepts.

2. Checks

a. Display Visual 4.3, *Checks*. Explain that this is a math exercise to demonstrate productivity. In this exercise, the students begin with a number and multiply it by 2 to get a product. Then, they multiply the product by 3, then by 4, and so on, until

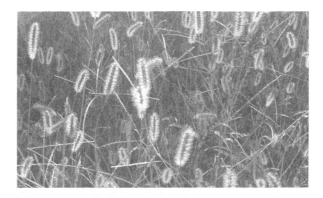

they reach the final multiplier assigned by the teacher. Then, they divide that final product by 2, then 3, then 4, and so on until they reach the number initially used in the multiplication. Point out this scheme on the visual.

b. Separate the students into pairs. Ask one student in each pair to act as timekeeper and one to volunteer to do a check. Depending on how much time you have available and the skill level of your students, give the volunteers a starting number of one or two digits and have them multiply and divide by a number between 5 and 10. Instruct each volunteer's partner to time him/her and record the number of minutes it takes the volunteer to complete the check correctly. DO NOT ALLOW CALCULATORS.

c. Explain to the students that they have applied skills they developed through education. Education is one way that people can increase their human capital.

d. When all volunteers have completed the check, instruct them to do the **exact** same problem again. Have timekeepers record the time it takes this time. The students will likely have completed the calculations in less time than in the first round.

e. Explain that the students were able to complete their calculations more quickly this time through practice. Human capital can be enhanced through practice. The more you practice a skill, the better you will become. Employers recognize this. When you are newly employed, your employer expects that you will need

39

time to develop your productivity. With practice doing the job, you will become more proficient.

f. Now offer the students calculators. Explain that you want to see the difference that capital investment can make in the students' productivity. Once again,

have the timekeepers record the time it takes their partners to complete the calculations. If time permits, allow the students to do this exercise twice, to demonstrate once again the value of practice in developing human capital.

COOL DOWN

Review the lesson by asking the following questions.

1. What is human capital? *(The combination of education, skills, and talents that enhances your value as a worker.)*

2. Why does investment in your human capital increase your possibility for greater future income? *(Employers are willing to pay more for skilled workers,* *because they are more productive.)*

3. How do capital resources increase productivity? *(Capital resources allow workers to get work done more efficiently.)*

4. How can you increase your human capital? *(Answers will vary, but the students should recognize that they must acquire education, practice their skills, and develop their talents.)*

Assessment

The students should complete Assessment Activity 4.1 in *Student Workouts* by researching a career choice. They should determine what skills are required of someone in that career, what capital resources are used in that career, and what level of income is associated with that occupational choice

Other Training Equipment

An annotated bibliography and Internet resources are available on our web site, **www.ncee.net**, as well as in *The Parents' Guide to Shaping Up Your Financial Future.*

Financial Fitness for Life: Shaping Up Your Financial Future Teacher Guide, ©National Council on Economic Education

Visual 4.1

The Story of Mike and Chris, Inc.

Mike and Chris had a grass-cutting business. Week after week, Mike and Chris cut the grass at a ball field. They had identical lawn mowers, began their cutting at the same time, and worked for two hours.

However, when they were through cutting the ball field, Mike had cut three-fourths of the field while Chris had cut only one-fourth. The ball field owner, Yolanda, commended Mike for his productivity.

Financial Fitness for Life: Shaping Up Your Financial Future Teacher Guide, ©National Council on Economic Education

Visual 4.2

Increasing Productivity of Workers

Use of capital resources

Capital resources are goods produced for the purpose of producing other goods and services. For instance, a hammer is a capital resource. A hammer is produced to aid in construction. It is much more effective than using a rock. A hammer increases the productivity of construction workers.

Investment in human capital

Human capital is the combination of education, skills, and talents a worker gathers over time. Knowing how to use new equipment (capital) and efficient procedures increases productivity. The development of your human capital enhances your value as a worker.

Visual 4.3

Checks

$2 \times 2 = 4$

$4 \times 3 = 12$

$12 \times 4 = 48$

$48 \times 5 = 240$

$240 \div 2 = 120$

$120 \div 3 = 40$

$40 \div 4 = 10$

$10 \div 5 = 2$

THEME 2

LESSON

5

Why Stay in School?

Fitness Focus

EQUIPMENT AND GETTING READY!

Make overhead transparencies of the visuals listed here.

✔ Visual 5.1, *Steps to Success*

✔ Visual 5.2, *Uneducated = Unemployed*

✔ Visual 5.3, *An Employer's Perspective*

✔ Introductory reading for Lesson 5 (*Shaping Up Your Financial Future Student Workouts*)

✔ Exercise 5.1, *Some Things About School Are So… (Shaping Up Your Financial Future Student Workouts)* (This is also used as a Parent Activity)

✔ Exercise 5.2, *Steps to Success (Shaping Up Your Financial Future Student Workouts)*

✔ Calculators (one per student)

✔ Unlined paper (one piece per student)

LESSON DESCRIPTION AND BACKGROUND

In this lesson, the students are encouraged to weigh costs and benefits when making decisions about education. The students will recognize that, on average, the higher the educational attainment, the greater the level of income one can expect. They will also discover that as people advance in their education, they are less likely to suffer unemployment.

This lesson is correlated with national standards for mathematics and economics as well as the national guidelines for personal financial management as shown in Tables 1 through 3 in the front of the book.

ECONOMIC AND PERSONAL FINANCE CONCEPTS

Income, opportunity cost, costs, benefits

Student Objectives

At the end of this lesson, the student will be able to:

✔ Explain the benefits associated with levels of educational attainment.

✔ Explain the costs associated with levels of educational attainment.

✔ Define *opportunity cost* and explain the opportunity cost of dropping out of school.

44

PARENT CONNECTION

There is no specific family activity worksheet for this lesson in *The Parents' Guide.*

Exercise 5.1, *Some Things About School Are So...* in *Student Workouts* asks for parental involvement in the exercise. The student is asked to describe school activities that range from easy to difficult. The students are to work with their parents to list ways the students could increase their aptitude in the areas that they find difficult. Ask the parents and students to work together on developing a plan of action, including a timetable for improvement.

The Parents' Guide is a tool for reinforcing and extending the instruction provided in the classroom. It includes:

1. Content background in the form of frequently asked questions.

2. Interesting activities that parents can do with their daughter or son.

3. An annotated listing of books and Internet resources related to each theme.

TIME REQUIRED 1 class period

Workout

WARM-UP

1. Begin the lesson by asking the students to draw a set of stairs, with at least five steps, from a side view. They should use only a pencil and unlined paper, no ruler or other guide. When they have completed their drawings, instruct them to use their rulers to measure the vertical distance between each step by measuring the riser for each step. Have them write the measurement of each step by the riser. Ask how many students drew a set of stairs where the riser measurements were the same for each step. (Concentrate on the number of students who have unequal risers.)

2. Ask all the students who think of school as an uphill climb to raise their hands. Explain that becoming educated *is* like climbing a set of stairs. However, the stairs the students climb to get an education are more like the stairs the students drew than the perfectly measured stairs we climb in our homes or in school. Some subjects in school and some levels of school take more effort; they require that we take bigger steps to reach the goal.

3. Instruct the students to take a brief self-inventory of the challenges they face in school. Refer them to Exercise 5.1, *Some Things About School Are So...* Direct the students to the columns headed, *Difficult, Comfortable,* and *Easy.* Under each column, have the students write any subjects, assignments, or skills related to their schoolwork that fall under these headings. For instance, some students might find math difficult, or may find just some area of math, such as word problems, difficult. They may find writing easy but the oral presentation of their writing to be difficult. They may have difficulty with personal traits, such as study skills. However, they may find neatness and organization easy to master. Help the students brainstorm as many areas as possible. Retain this sheet for the assessment and the parent involvement.

4. Explain that just as certain subject areas and certain tasks may be difficult, comfortable, or easy, different levels of education may also be more difficult than others; however, each level brings rewards.

45

5. Have the students take home the completed Exercise 5.1 to show their parents. Ask each student to work with his or her parent to develop a plan to deal with the difficult school aspects. A written report could be required.

EXERCISE

1. Have students read the *Warm-Up, Fitness Vocabulary, Muscle Developers*, and *Showing Your Strength* of Lesson 5 in *Student Workouts*. Focus on any concepts that are difficult for the students to understand.

2. Steps to Success

a. Display Visual 5.1, *Steps to Success*, and explain that this set of stairs represents different levels of educational attainment and the median income associated with each level. Note that the median level of income increases with each step, as do the students' knowledge and abilities.

b. Refer the students to Exercise 5.2, *Steps to Success* in *Student Workouts*, and ask them to complete question 1, which asks the students to calculate the difference in median income between each level of educational attainment *(a. $7,332; b. $4,732; c. $11,856; and d. $11,804).* Point out that this is an annual difference. For instance, someone with a bachelor's degree earns, on average, $11,856 more every year than the person with an associate's degree.

c. Note that the median level of income for a high school dropout is $18,876. Point out that this doesn't mean that someone who drops out of school at age 16 will earn $18,876. The *median wage* (for all working

people without a high school diploma) means that half of those people earn more than this amount and half earn less than this amount.

d. Explain that at a certain age, depending on your state laws, the students can choose to get off the steps. They can simply stop at the first step, after completing, say, the tenth grade, and move into the labor force. Or they can continue, step by step, to reach some other goal. Each step represents a benefit as well as a cost.

e. Define *marginal benefit* as the additional benefit that would be obtained from one more unit of some good or service. In the case of education, the marginal benefit could be the additional income per year that would result from one more year of education. The marginal benefit of education could also be measured by the attainment of additional skills that could result in additional challenges or additional job satisfaction. Point out that this marginal benefit would occur for every year of their working life.

f. Refer the students back to Exercise 5.2. Instruct them to calculate the lifetime earnings at each level of educational attainment (Question 2). Answers are in the table below.

Answers for calculation of lifetime earnings at different levels of education.

	H.S. dropout	H.S. diploma	Associate's degree	Bachelor's degree	Advanced degree
Annual Income	$18,876	$26,208	$30,940	$42,796	$54,600
Years worked	54	52	50	48	46
Life earnings	$1,019,304	$1,362,816	$1,547,000	$2,054,208	$2,511,600

Financial Fitness for Life: Shaping Up Your Financial Future Teacher Guide, ©National Council on Economic Education

g. Direct the students' attention to someone who has dropped out of high school after tenth grade and someone who has graduated from high school. Assuming a working life of 52 years for the high school graduate and 54 years for the dropout, the students should find that the dropout's lifetime earnings is $1,019,304 (54 × 18,876), while the high school graduate's lifetime earnings is $1,362,816 (52 × 26,208). Ask the students to state the difference in lifetime earnings ($343,512). Explain that the cost of dropping out of school is the difference in lifetime earnings. In this case, it is $343,512, or approximately a 25 percent drop (343,512 ÷ 1,362,816) in lifetime earnings for the high school dropout.

h. Explain an even more distressing point about high school dropouts; they are twice as likely to be unemployed. Direct the students to Visual 5.2, *Uneducated = Unemployed*. Explain that these are the 2000 United States average unemployment rates by educational attainment. Ask the students to note the unemployment rate for people who attended only one-to-three years of high school and compare that figure with the unemployment rate for high school graduates. Ask the students to speculate as to why the unemployment rate would be so much higher for those who had not completed high school. Prompt the students by asking what an employer's impression of a high school dropout might be.

i. Display Visual 5.3, *An Employer's Perspective*. Ask the students if these are fair assessments on the employer's part. *(The students will likely indicate these assessments are unfair.)* Allow discussion, but explain that in the final analysis, employers have little to go on when hiring someone. So they use certain measures, such as educational attainment, to determine who is likely to be a good employee. If a high school graduate and a high school dropout apply for the same job, and if their other attributes, such as skills or work experience, are equal, it is almost

a certainty that the high school graduate will get the job.

j. Explain that the class has examined the benefits of staying in school, but they should know that there are also costs. Ask the following questions:

▲ **What full-time jobs might be available to someone who is 17 years old?** *(Retail clerk, fast food worker, car wash worker, etc.)*

▲ **What is the average hourly wage paid to people starting in those positions?** *(Answers will vary, but the students should recognize that wage rates for these jobs vary from minimum wage to $8.00 per hour.)*

k. Explain that at 40 hours per week, and 52 weeks per year, it is possible to work 2,080 hours per year. Tell the students to use the most optimistic point of this wage range, $8.00 per hour, and calculate the annual income. (2,080 × 8 = $16,640)

l. Explain that people use money and time to obtain additional education. Allocating money and time to education involves opportunity cost. Define *opportunity cost* as the next-best forgone alternative when a decision is made. The year's salary is the opportunity cost, or income forgone, if you attend school full time for the year.

47

m. Tell the students to assume the same wage for a second year and ask the opportunity cost of finishing high school ($16,640 + 16,640 = $33,280.) Ask the students to recall that a high school graduate will earn an average of $343,512 more than the dropout over a lifetime, and will work two fewer years. Ask the students whether the costs outweigh the benefits, or do the benefits outweigh the costs.

n. Explain that as the students move on to college, the costs become significantly higher. Annual tuition costs can range from about $8,000 at a public university to $18,000 or more at a private university. These figures do not include housing costs, because such costs occur regardless of whether the student is in school or not. Ask the students whether there are any other costs that must be considered when calculating the cost of attending a two-year college as a full-time student. *(Amount of forgone income that could be earned.)*

o. Refer the students to Visual 5.1. Explain that as people increase their educational attainment they also increase their income. Ask the students why the additional income could be important. *(Answers will vary. Guide the students to recognize that greater income allows them more goods and services, more choices, and greater financial security.)* Explain that higher educational attainment, in general, brings about greater income, which then brings about a higher standard of living. Also, greater educational attainment can bring about greater job satisfaction. People who have reached high levels of education generally have more choices in jobs.

COOL DOWN

1. Reinforce the concepts discussed in this lesson by asking the following questions:

a. At what level of educational attainment is there likely to be the greatest level of unemployment? *(The level of the high school dropout.)*

b. Why is the unemployment rate so much higher for the high school dropout? *(Answers will vary, but the students should recognize that the high school dropout is likely to be unskilled and that employers are less likely to believe a high school dropout can face the challenges of a job.)*

c. What are the benefits associated with increasing educational attainment? *(Greater income, higher standard of living, greater job satisfaction, more choices.)*

d. As people consider the benefits of increasing their educational attainment what must they also consider? *(The costs.)*

e. What is opportunity cost? *(The next-best forgone alternative.)*

f. What is the opportunity cost of staying in high school until graduation? *(The wages that could have been earned during that period.)*

g. In addition to forgone wages, what are some additional costs to attend college? *(Costs of tuition, fees, books, and supplies.)*

Assessment

1. Refer the student to Exercise 5.1, Some Things About *Schoolwork are So...* Explain to the students that their list in the "Easy" column probably contains their special aptitudes and skills. Using the information in this column, ask each student to write a list of occupations that require aptitude in the skills the student listed. Instruct the students to choose one of those occupations and write a brief essay stating the following:

a. the level of education required for this occupation,

b. the costs of obtaining the education required in terms of time spent and lost earnings, and,

c. the expected benefits in terms of financial rewards and fulfillment.

2. The students can research the *Occupational Outlook Handbook* at **http://stats.bls.gov/ocohome.htm**. They may also discover the information they need by interviewing someone in the occupation they are considering.

Other Training Equipment

An annotated bibliography and Internet resources are available on our web site, **www.ncee.net**, or in *The Parents' Guide to Shaping Up Your Financial Future*.

49

Visual 5.1

Steps to Success

(Median earnings of full-time wage and salary workers.)

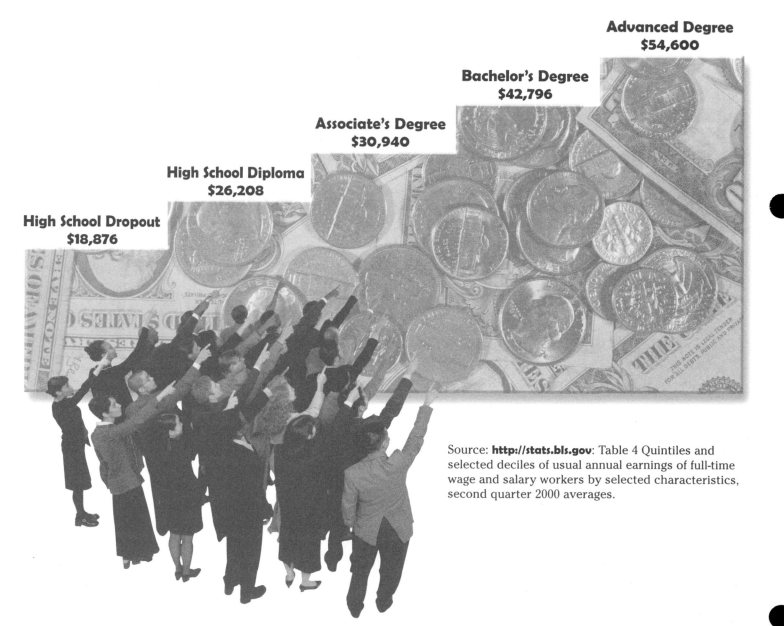

Advanced Degree
$54,600

Bachelor's Degree
$42,796

Associate's Degree
$30,940

High School Diploma
$26,208

High School Dropout
$18,876

Source: **http://stats.bls.gov**: Table 4 Quintiles and selected deciles of usual annual earnings of full-time wage and salary workers by selected characteristics, second quarter 2000 averages.

Financial Fitness for Life: Shaping Up Your Financial Future Teacher Guide, ©National Council on Economic Education

Visual 5.2

Uneducated = Unemployed

**Unemployment rates
by educational level**

Less than a high school diploma. . . 6.1%

High school diploma, no college 3.7%

Some college 2.9%

College graduate 1.8%

Source: **www.bls.gov**: Table A-3, Employment statistics of the civilian population
25 years and over by educational attainment August 2000.

Visual 5.3

An Employer's Perspective

"Someone who couldn't complete high school probably finds it difficult to complete any task."

"High school can be hard work. A high school dropout is probably scared of a little hard work."

"How bright can a high school dropout be?"

"A high school dropout didn't learn some things that are needed to be good at this job."

THEME 3

LESSON

6

Why Save?

Fitness Focus

EQUIPMENT AND GETTING READY!

Make overhead transparencies of the visuals listed here.

✔ Visual 6.1, *Short-, Medium-, and Long-Term Goals and Opportunity Cost*

✔ Visual 6.2, *Why It's Harder to Save for Long-Term Goals than for Short-Term Goals*

✔ Activity 6.1, *Game Cards for Rolling for a Goal*

✔ Introductory reading for Theme 3 and Lesson 6 (*Shaping Up Your Financial Future Student Workouts*)

✔ Exercise 6.1, *How To Reach A Goal* (*Shaping Up Your Financial Future Student Workouts*)

✔ Exercise 6.2, *Rolling For A Goal, A Game for Two or More Players* (*Shaping Up Your Financial Future Student Workouts*)

✔ Assessment 6.1, *Short-, Medium-, and Long-Term Goals* (*Shaping Up Your Financial Future Student Workouts*)

✔ Family Activity 5, *Savings and Goals* (*The Parents' Guide for Shaping Up Your Financial Future*)

✔ Scissors and a pair of dice for each group of four students

✔ Three 4" x 6" index cards for each student

✔ Sticky note or index cards

LESSON DESCRIPTION

In this lesson, the students learn about saving and investing, and they consider the importance of setting short-term, medium-term, and long-term savings goals. They use math skills to solve problems and they play a game called "Rolling For a Goal" to reinforce the concept of goal setting and working towards a goal. Finally, they engage in a family activity that focuses on the opportunity cost of saving.

This lesson is correlated with national standards for mathematics and economics as well as the national guidelines for personal financial management as shown in Tables 1 through 3 in the front of the book.

ECONOMIC AND PERSONAL FINANCE CONCEPTS

Short-term goals, medium-term goals, long-term goals, opportunity cost

Student Objectives

At the end of this lesson, the student will be able to:

✔ Recognize the importance of goal-setting.

✔ Define short-term, medium-term, and long-term goals.

✔ Use math to project savings goals.

✔ Identify the opportunity cost of saving.

53

PARENT CONNECTION

Family Activity 5, *Saving and Goals*, asks the family to list some short-, medium-, and long-term goals that they have. The family is also asked to identify what they give up if they save toward each of these goals. There is a case problem also, *Test Your Financial Fitness*, in this family activity. Some answers include:

(This is a long-term goal because it will take six years to achieve [You are 15 and you want to save for the down payment on a house when you are 21.] You will not have enough money; you need $1400 more.

Explanation: 6 years × 52 weeks = 312 weeks to save. 312 weeks × $300 per week = $93,600

saved altogether. Ten per cent of $950,000 is $95,000 needed for down payment. $95,000 – $93,600 = $1,400 more is needed.)*

The Parents' Guide is a tool for reinforcing and extending the instruction provided in the classroom. It includes:

1. Content background in the form of frequently asked questions.

2. Interesting activities that parents can do with their daughter or son.

3. An annotated listing of books and Internet resources related to each theme.

Workout

WARM-UP

1. Introduce the idea of goal setting by asking the students what steps they would take in a campaign to run for student council president. Remind the students that some campaign activities take place months before the election, while others must be completed just weeks or days prior to the voting.

   a. Divide the class into small groups and allow about 10 minutes for each group to brainstorm ideas about "Things To Do To Prepare For An Election Campaign," recording each idea on a sticky note or index card (one idea per note).

   b. On the board, draw five large circles, labeling them, from left to right, "Three months before election," "One month before election," 'Two weeks before election," "One week before election," "One day before election."

   c. Invite the students to post their notes on the board in the appropriate circles.

d. Discuss reasons for the students' responses.

2. Explain that, like a campaign, saving for a goal also requires planning.

   a. Ask the students what saving money means. *(Putting money aside from current income to buy something in the future.)*

   b. Explain that people can save money in a jar at home or they can save in a bank or another financial institution. *(When people save in a bank, their money earns interest. The money they save becomes an investment; they will eventually have more dollars and cents than they deposited.)*

   c. Ask why people save money. *(To get goods and services in the future that they may not be able to afford now, to have an emergency fund in case some catastrophe occurs, and to have money in the future for retirement when they are no longer working.)*

54

d. Ask if any students are currently saving money and why they are saving?
(Answers will vary.)

e. Explain that saving money requires short-term, medium-term and long-term planning.

EXERCISE

1. Short-, Medium-, and Long-Term Goals

a. Display Visual 6.1, *Short-, Medium- and Long-Term Goals and Opportunity Cost*, and review definitions with the class. Ask the students to suggest goods or services whose purchase might require short-, medium- or long-term savings goals. *(Answers will vary. Accept any reasonable responses.)*

b. Have the students explain why a short-term goal for one saver might be a long-term goal for another. *(The amount that can be saved in any time period varies depending upon an individual's income, earnings, and expenses.)*

c. Display Visual 6.2, *Why It's Harder to Save for Long-Term Goals Than for Short-Term Goals.*

d. Explain that long-term goals are usually more difficult to meet than are short-term goals. When a person is saving for more than three years, there is more time for emergencies or consumer expenditures to present themselves before the savings goal is met. If the emergency or the expenditure is valued more highly than the savings goal, the goal may be abandoned in favor of the other alternative. In economic terms, the opportunity cost of saving might be greater than the opportunity cost of the emergency expenditure.

e. Explain that saving goals depend upon how much has to be saved and how much time is available for saving.

f. Have the students read the *Introduction* to Theme 3 and the *Warm-Up* and *Fitness Vocabulary* of Lesson 6 in *Student Workouts*. Discuss the new vocabulary, making sure the students understand the concepts.

g. Have the students finish reading *Muscle Developers* and *Showing Your Strength* in *Student Workouts* and independently complete Exercise 6.1, *How To Reach A Goal*. Review the answers that are given on the next page.

h. Define *opportunity cost* as the next-best alternative that is given up when a choice is made.

i. Explain that when people choose to save for the future, they give up the chance to spend in the present. The alternative they give up is their opportunity cost.

j. Review the problems in Exercise 6.1, asking the students to identify the opportunity cost in each problem. *(When José, Lauren, and Darnell decided to save for the future, they gave up the chance to spend in the present.)*

2. Rolling for a Goal.

a. Divide the class into groups of four. Before starting the exercise, make sufficient sets of Activity Sheet 6.1 *Game Cards for Rolling for a Goal* so each group has a set. Give a set of game cards and two dice to each group.

b. Have the students turn to Exercise 6.2, *Rolling For A Goal*. Instruct the students to follow the game directions, being sure to identify goals as short-, medium-, or long-term on their score sheet.

c. After the game is finished, engage the students in a discussion of the differences among short-, medium-, and long-term saving goals. *(The students should recognize that goals can be short-, medium-, or long-term depending upon the amount of money to be saved and the amount that can be saved during a specific period, i.e., week, month, year, etc.)*

d. Ask the students if leaving a saving goal to chance (the roll of a die) is a good idea. *(The students should recognize that many of the goals were not met when they did not save enough each month or long enough—factors that were determined by the roll of the dice.)*

55

ANSWERS (to Exercise 6.1, How to Reach a Goal)

▲ *It will take Jose a little over three years to save enough for the bracelet. This is a long-term goal. Explanation: Jose earns $36 a week; he saves $15 for college and spends $8; $15 + $8 = $23. That leaves $13 every week to save for the bracelet. ($36 − $23 = $13). The bracelet costs $2100. $2100 ÷ $13 = 161.5 weeks to save. 161.5 divided by 52 weeks in a year = 3.1 years. If Jose saves his money in an interest-bearing bank account, he will meet his goal earlier.*

▲ *It will take Lauren 7.95 weeks to save for the saxophone. This is a short-term goal. Explanation: Lauren saves $5.00 of her allowance money for college. That leaves $22 every week ($17 from baby sitting and $5 from allowance) for the saxophone. The saxophone costs $175. $175 ÷ $22 = 7.95 weeks, not quite 2 months.*

▲ *Darnell will not be able to save enough money for his short-term goal. He earns $75 per week, saves $20, gives $5 to charity, and spends $8. That means he has $42 per week for the golf lessons ($75 − $20 − $5 − $8 = $42). In six weeks he'll have only $252 ($42 × 6). He needs $48 more for the golf lessons. Answers will vary as to how Darnell could change his saving or spending plan in order to meet his goal. Some of the discussion should focus on the importance of giving and sharing as part of a total savings/spending plan.*

COOL DOWN

▲ Distribute three 4" × 6" index cards to each student.

▲ Have the students make up three math problems (similar to those in Exercise 6.1) about short-, medium-, and long-term goals.

▲ The students should write one problem on each card, with answers on the back.

▲ When all the problems are written, put the cards in a box so the students can challenge each other.

Assessment

Distribute Assessment 6.1 *Short-, Medium-, and Long-Term Goals (Shaping Up Your Financial Future Student Workouts)* to the students at the completion of the lesson. The answer key is at the end of this lesson.

Other Training Equipment

An annotated bibliography and Internet resources can be found on our web site, **www.ncee.net**, and in *The Parents' Guide to Shaping Up Your Financial Future*.

Visual 6.1

Short-, Medium-, and Long-Term Goals and Opportunity Cost

Short-term savings goals can be achieved in fewer than two months.

Medium-term savings goals may take from 2 months to 3 years to achieve.

Long-term savings goals require 3 years or more to achieve.

Saving for the future means giving up the opportunity to spend in the present.

The next-best alternative that is given up when saving for a goal is called the opportunity cost.

Visual 6.2

Why It's Harder to Save for Long-Term Goals Than for Short-Term Goals

It is harder to save for long-term than for short-term goals. If you are saving for the long term, it's more likely that something might come along that you'll value more highly than your savings goal.

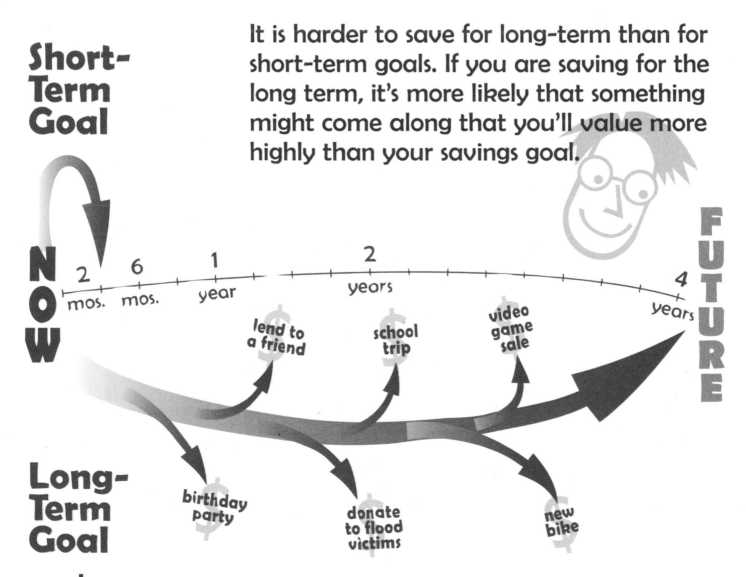

ACTIVITY 6.1

Game Cards for Rolling For a Goal

These are the saving goals for Exercise 6.2, **Rolling for a Goal.**
Photocopy this page to make one set for each group of four in your class. Cut
apart, shuffle and place face down in a pile in front of the players in each group.

Mountain bike $300	New computer system $1500	New stereo set-up $1600	One casual clothing outfit $120
Inline skates $200	Collection of CDs $700	New furniture for your room $2500	Drum set $2000
Spending money for class trip $150	Snowboard and boots $500	Tennis lessons from a Pro $1000	Airfare to visit grandparents $400
Family trip to Disney World $2400	Annual family membership in health club $1600	Big screen TV for your bedroom $1900	Saddle and tack for horse $1700
Clothing shopping spree $600	Cell phone and annual calling costs $600	Two tickets to a professional basketball game $120	Aquarium and fish $200
	Leather jacket $700	Collection of CDs and DVDs $1200	

Financial Fitness for Life: Shaping Up Your Financial Future Teacher Guide, ©National Council on Economic Education

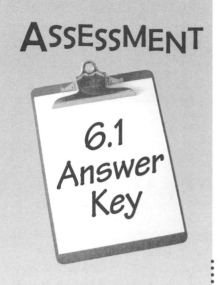

ASSESSMENT

6.1
Answer
Key

Short-, Medium-, and Long-Term Goals

Use Assessment 6.1 to determine whether the students have mastered the concepts in this lesson. Answers are provided in the chart below:

Person	Amount to be saved	Amount saved each month	How many months?	How many years?	Short-, medium- or long-term?
Abby	$780.00	$20.00	39.00	3.25	L
Ben	$25.00	$15.00	1.67	0.14	S
Cherise	$700.00	$35.00	20.00	1.67	M
Danuka	$800.00	$70.00	11.43	0.95	M
Emilio	$90.00	$50.00	1.80	0.15	S
Festis	$2900.00	$75.00	38.67	3.22	L

(It will take Cherise 20 months to reach her savings goal of $700.

The opportunity cost of saving for the future is the chance to spend money in the present. Accept any reasonable answer for each month's opportunity cost. Examples: January opportunity cost = noisemakers and party hats for New Year's Party; February opportunity cost = red sweater for Valentine's Day; June opportunity cost = beverages and snacks for end-of-the-school-year picnic; July opportunity cost = flags, hot dogs, and apple pie for July Fourth celebration; September opportunity cost = pens, rulers and notebooks for back-to-school; October opportunity cost = pumpkins and costume for Halloween party; December opportunity cost = woolen hat and gloves for ski trip.)

Financial Fitness for Life: Shaping Up Your Financial Future Teacher Guide, ©National Council on Economic Education

THEME 3

LESSON

7

Types of Savings Plans

Fitness Focus

EQUIPMENT AND GETTING READY!

✔ Introductory reading for Lesson 7 (*Shaping Up Your Financial Future Student Workouts*)

✔ Exercise 7.1, *Types of Guaranteed Savings Instruments* (*Shaping Up Your Financial Future Student Workouts*)

✔ Exercise 7.2, *Savings Plans in My Community* (*Shaping Up Your Financial Future Student Workouts*)

✔ Assessment 7.1, *Types of Savings Plans* (*Shaping Up Your Financial Future Student Workouts*)

TIME REQUIRED
1 class period.

LESSON DESCRIPTION AND BACKGROUND

In this lesson, the students learn about the various types of government insured savings instruments, and the advantages and disadvantages of each.

ECONOMIC AND PERSONAL FINANCE CONCEPTS

Portfolio, savings instrument, savings account, certificate of deposit, money market deposit account, U.S. Savings Bond

This lesson is correlated with national standards for mathematics and economics as well as the national guidelines for personal financial management as shown in Tables 1 through 3 in the front of the book.

Student Objectives

At the end of this lesson, the student will be able to:

✔ Define savings instruments.

✔ Name the advantages and disadvantages of various savings instruments.

✔ Select a savings instrument which best meets one's needs at a particular time.

✔ Explain why it is important to shop around for savings instruments.

61

PARENT CONNECTION

There is no specific family activity worksheet for this lesson but there are activities in *The Parents' Guide* that parents may want to use with this lesson. They can be found in the "Raising the Bar" section for Theme 3.

The Parents' Guide is a tool for reinforcing and extending the instruction provided in the classroom. It includes:

1. Content background in the form of frequently asked questions.
2. Interesting activities that parents can do with their son or daughter.
3. An annotated listing of books and Internet resources related to each theme.

Workout

WARM-UP

1. Introduce the lesson by saying that a savings instrument is a tool people have for saving their money for future purchases. Often, people save to make small and large purchases in the future, for example, an appliance, a stereo, a house, car, or college education for the kids. However, people also save for emergencies or to have a source of income during retirement.

2. Introduce the concept of *risk*. Risk refers to the possibility of loss. Insurance guarantees the safety of your money in different savings instruments in most banks. You cannot lose your deposit, even if the bank goes out of business. The Federal Deposit Insurance Corporation (FDIC) insures your deposits up to $100,000 in a bank that displays their logo. The National Credit Union Association (NCUA) does the same for credit unions.

3. Explain that there are nearly as many ways to save as there are reasons to save. All of the various types of savings instruments can make choosing the best method very confusing because there is no one best method. Individuals have different incomes, different saving goals, and a different time line to meet their goals. Individuals should familiarize themselves with the various plans and choose those that will best meet their needs.

4. Define *portfolio* as a person's financial security "package" or collection. Point out that this package or portfolio should include a variety of savings and investment instruments. In other words, it should be *diversified*.

5. Explain that in later lessons, the students will learn about many other methods to build financial security for the future. In addition to traditional saving instruments, people can place money in investment instruments such as stocks, corporate bonds, or mutual funds. Each saving and investment instrument has advantages and disadvantages. In this lesson, the students learn about traditional savings instruments.

EXERCISE

1. Ask the students to name all the saving or investment methods they've heard of and write the list on the board. Circle those that are commonly offered by banks, savings and loan associations, and credit unions. These would include the savings account, the certificate of deposit, the money market deposit account, and the U.S. Savings Bond. These are the tools people can use to save money; in other words, these are *savings instruments.*

2. Have the students read the *Warm-Up, Fitness Vocabulary, Muscle Developers, Showing Your Strength,* and Exercise 7.1, *Types of Guaranteed Saving Instruments* in *Student Workouts.* Discuss the definitions as well as the advantages and disadvantages of each type of saving method as follows. After discussing the various types, have the students answer the six questions that appear at the end of the exercise. *(Answers: 1.) Statement savings account; 2.) CD with duration of less than three years; money market deposit account, or statement savings account; 3.) money market deposit account or statement savings account; 4.) Money market deposit account or statement savings account; 5.) CD; 6.) U.S. Savings Bonds.)*

3. Review the point that every saving decision has an opportunity cost. *Opportunity cost is the second best alternative that is given up when a choice must be made.* The person who decides to save gives up the item that he or she could have purchased with that money now.

4. Instruct the students to think about the types of saving methods they have been learning about and answer the following questions.

a. If a person saves $1,000, what is the opportunity cost? *(It is what the saver could have bought currently for $1,000.)*

b. If a person saves $1,000 in a Series EE Savings Bond rather than a statement savings account, what is the opportunity cost? *(It is access to the money for a period of time without penalty [loss of interest.])*

c. If a person decides to save $1,000 in a twelve-month CD rather than in a statement savings account, what is the opportunity cost? *(It is the access to the money without penalty during the 12 months.)*

d. If that person decides to save $1,000 in a regular savings account rather than in a CD, what is the opportunity cost? *(It is the higher interest rate he or she would have had on the savings in a CD.)*

5. Local Savings Plans

a. Indicate that saving plans can vary quite a bit from one financial institution to another. Assign the students to work in groups to visit local banks, savings and loans or credit unions to obtain information about savings plans at each institution.

b. Have the students use Exercise 7.2 to record their findings.

c. Ask each group to present their findings to the class, and consolidate those findings on an overhead transparency.

d. Discuss the similarities and differences the students find among banks and savings and loans and credit unions. Which institution had the best rates of interest for savers? Were penalties the same in all institutions?

63

COOL DOWN

Review the concepts taught in this lesson by asking the following questions.

1. **What are some of the advantages of a money market deposit account?** *(The saver usually can write checks on the account; the account is insured up to $100,000; the interest rate increases as the market interest rates increase.)*

2. **What are some of the disadvantages of a money market deposit account?** *(The saver must maintain a substantial minimum balance. The interest rate may be lower than in other options.)*

3. **What are some of the advantages of a statement savings account?** *(The saver can withdraw the money as needed; the interest rate increases as the market rates increase; the saver can maintain small balances.)*

4. **What are some of the disadvantages of a statement savings account?** *(Statement savings accounts usually pay a lower interest rate than other options. Rates will decrease as the market interest rates decrease.)*

5. **What are some of the advantages of a certificate of deposit?** *(CDs pay a higher interest rate than regular savings accounts; the interest rate is "locked in" so if market interest rates go down, the saver continues to get the higher rate until the CD expires.)*

6. **What are the disadvantages of a certificate of deposit?** *(The saver cannot withdraw money from a CD without significant penalty until the CD has expired; the interest rate is locked in so that if the market interest rate goes up, the CD holder is stuck with the lower interest rate.)*

7. **What are the advantages of U.S. Savings Bonds?** *(Small amounts of money can be saved with U.S. Savings Bonds; the U.S. government guarantees them; they usually pay a higher rate of interest than regular savings accounts; possible tax advantages.)*

8. **What is the disadvantage of U.S. Savings Bonds?** *(There is a penalty [loss of some interest] if they are cashed before maturity.)*

Assessment

Have the students complete Assessment 7.1.

Answers: *1. A; 2. D; 3. A or C; 4. B; 5. A or C.*

Other Training Equipment

An annotated bibliography and listing of additional Internet resources are available on our web site, **www.ncee.net**, and in *The Parents' Guide* for *Shaping Up Your Financial Future.*

Financial Fitness for Life: Shaping Up Your Financial Future Teacher Guide, ©National Council on Economic Education

LESSON
8

Who Pays and Who Receives?

Fitness Focus

Make overhead transparencies of the visuals listed here.

✔ Visual 8.1, *Interesting Information About Interest*

✔ Visuals 8.2A, *Simple Interest* and 8.2B *Compound Interest*

✔ Visuals 8.3A and 8.3B, *Answers*

✔ Visual 8.4, *Factors That Affect How Money Grows*

All readings, exercises, and the assessment are in *Shaping Up Your Financial Future Student Workouts*

✔ Introductory reading for Lesson 8

✔ Exercise 8.1A, *Simple Interest*

✔ Exercise 8.1B, *Compound Interest*

✔ Exercise 8.2, *Simple Interest: When and Why Would People Choose It?*

✔ Exercise 8.3, *Racing Toward a Goal*

✔ Exercise 8.4, *Checking Out the Rule of 72: Does It Work?*

✔ Assessment 8.1 *Factors that Affect How Money Grows*

✔ Family Activity 6, *The Power of Compounding (The Parents' Guide for Shaping Up Your Financial Future)*

✔ Bag of large dried kidney beans (or other beans.)

✔ Two tall, narrow glass jars (labeled *Simple* and *Compound*).

✔ One small narrow glass jar (labeled *Interest Paid Out To Depositor*).

✔ Two overhead projectors

✔ Calculators (one for each student)

LESSON DESCRIPTION

In this lesson, students learn that banks are businesses and, as such, seek to make a profit. One way banks do this is by charging borrowers a higher rate of interest than the interest that is paid to savers. Students discover that three factors affect how money grows: amount deposited, interest rate, and time. Students calculate interest—both simple and compound—and they formulate a generalization about the difference between simple and compound interest. Finally, they engage in a family activity using the Rule of 72 to estimate how long it takes for money to double.

This lesson is correlated with national standards for mathematics and economics as well as the national guidelines for personal financial management as shown in Tables 1 through 3 in the front of the book.

ECONOMIC AND PERSONAL FINANCE CONCEPTS

Interest, interest rate, simple interest, compound interest, compounding, opportunity cost, rule of 72

Student Objectives

At the end of this lesson, the student will be able to:

✔ Explain how banks make a profit.

✔ Calculate simple and compound interest.

✔ Explain the opportunity cost of not allowing interest to compound; explain the opportunity cost of not taking interest as it is earned.

✔ Analyze the difference between simple and compound interest.

✔ Explain the factors that affect how money grows.

✔ Apply the Rule of 72.

PARENT CONNECTION

Family Activity 6 in *The Parents' Guide* shows the principle supporting compound interest. This is an important principle for both students and their parents to understand.

The Parents' Guide is a tool for reinforcing and extending the instruction provided in the classroom. It includes:

1. Content background in the form of frequently asked questions.

2. Interesting activities that parents can do with their son or daughter.

3. An annotated listing of books and Internet resources related to each theme.

TIME REQUIRED 3 to 4 class periods

Workout

WARM-UP

1. Introduce the concept of *interest* by asking if any students have savings accounts. If they do, ask why they keep their money in a savings account instead of in a dresser drawer or a shoebox in their closets. *(Some students will undoubtedly know that banks provide security and pay interest on savings; discuss these concepts to make sure students understand them.)*

2. Display Visual 8.1 *Interesting Information About Interest* and discuss the definitions.

Make sure students understand the difference between simple and compound interest.

3. Explain that when people leave their interest in the bank, it usually compounds, and savings grow rapidly.

4. Explain that sometimes people need their interest to pay for goods and services. They may not be able to leave all of it in the bank to compound; consequently their savings grow more slowly.

EXERCISE

1. Simple Interest and Compound Interest.

a. Explain that students will participate in a simulation that demonstrates the difference between simple and compound interest.

b. Divide the class into two groups: *Simple Interest Group* and *Compound Interest Group.* Have students turn to Exercise 8.1A and B in *Student Workouts.* Students in the *Simple Interest Group* use Exercise 8.1A, *Simple Interest;* the *Compound Interest Group* uses Exercise 8.1B, *Compound Interest.*

c. Give the one narrow, tall jar labeled *Simple Interest* and the smaller jar labeled *Interest Paid Out to Depositor* to the

Simple Interest Group. Give the tall, narrow jar labeled *Compound Interest* to the *Compound Interest Group.*

d. Display transparencies of Visual 8.2A and 8.2B, *Simple and Compound Interest,* side-by-side on the two overhead projectors.

e. Choose two students, one from each group, to act as bankers. Give each banker a bag of beans. Have each banker count 10 beans from the 'bank bag' into his or her group's jar labeled *Simple Interest* or *Compound Interest.* Have the rest of the students note the deposit in Column C of their respective charts; point this out on the visuals.

f. Tell the students that the interest rate is 20 percent interest, which is a high rate of interest, but it will make the calculations easier, and not affect the concept to be learned.

g. Instruct both bankers to take two beans from their respective bags to represent the 20% interest. The *Simple Interest* banker should put the two beans in the jar marked "Interest Paid Out To Depositor." The *Compound Interest* banker puts two beans in the same jar with the original deposit. *(20 percent of 10 = .2 × 10 = 2)*

h. Explain that when interest is allowed to *compound*, it is added to the existing balance and also earns interest. When interest is paid out to the depositor, it does not compound.

i. Have both groups look at their ending balance (column G). Because the *Compound Interest Group* kept its interest on deposit, it has 12 beans while the *Simple Interest Group* has only 10.

j. Continue to work through the deposit cycle again. Have student complete 6 cycles. (Deposit 10 beans, calculate interest, add 'interest beans' to correct jar.) Have each group calculate its new balance (Column D), interest earned (Column F) and ending balance (Column G). You can complete the visuals as the students calculate each cycle.

k. Have the students count the beans in the compound interest jar (there should be 119) and in the two jars for the simple interest group. (They should have 60 beans in the deposit jar, and 42 beans in the interest paid out, for a total of 102.) Double check their answers by having the students calculate the total amount deposited in column C, and the total interest earned in column F.

l. Display Visuals 8.3A and B, *Answer Sheets* (or use the transparency you have with the written answers.) Note that the *Simple Interest Group* and the *Compound Interest Group* each deposited the same amount, 60 beans. However, the *Compound Interest Group* earned a total of 59 beans in interest,

but the *Simple Interest Group* earned only 42 beans.

m. Ask the students what the opportunity cost was when *Simple Interest Group* chose to receive its interest instead of re-depositing it. *(The opportunity cost was the extra interest they would have earned.)*

n. Ask what the opportunity cost of the Compound Interest Group was. *(By saving all their interest for the future, their opportunity cost was not being able to spend the interest in the present.)* Remind students that, at times, savers cannot take advantage of compounding because they must use their accumulated interest to pay for the goods and services they want.

2. Have the students read the *Warm-Up* and *Fitness Vocabulary* for Lesson 8 from *Student Workouts.* Discuss the readings.

▲ Ask the students why banks charge a higher interest rate to borrowers than they pay to savers. *(Answer: Banks are businesses. Banks must charge a higher interest rate to borrowers than the interest rate they pay to savers to cover expenses and earn profit.)*

▲ Make sure students understand the new concepts and glossary terms.

3. Have students read *Muscle Developers* and *Showing Your Strength* in *Student Workouts.* Discuss any concepts or ideas that the students have difficulty in understanding.

4. Emphasize the factors that affect the amount of interest gained from a saving plan.

a. Display Visual 8.4, *Factors that Affect How Money Grows*, making sure students understand how the amount of savings, time, and interest rate impact the interest earned.

b. Have students independently or in pairs, complete Exercise 8.2, *Simple Interest: When and Why Would People Choose It?* Answers are given on the next page:

Exercise 8.2 Answers

Principal	×	Interest Rate	×	Time	=	Simple Interest	÷ 4 =	Quarterly Payment
$60,000	×	6%	×	1 Year	=	$3,600	÷ 4 =	$900
$20,000	×	5%	×	1 Year	=	**$1,000**	÷ 4 =	**$250**
$10,000	×	10%	×	1 Year	=	$1,000	÷ 4 =	**$250**
$80,000	×	**7%**	×	1 Year	=	$5,600	÷ 4 =	**$1,400**
$75,000	×	9%	×	1 Year	=	**$6,750**	÷ 4 =	**$1,688**
$125,000	×	8%	×	1 Year =		**$10,000**	÷ 4 =	**$2,500**
$200,000	×	**7%**	×	1 Year	=	$14,000	÷ 4 =	**$3,500**
$40,000	×	**5%**	×	1 Year	=	**$2,000**	÷ 4 =	$500
$100,000	×	4%	×	1 Year	=	**$4,000**	÷ 4 =	$1,000
$100,000	×	**10%**	×	1 Year	=	**$10,000**	÷ 4 =	$2,500

5. Racing Toward a Goal: The effect of time, interest rate, and amount saved on interest earned.

a. Explain that this exercise will demonstrate how money grows at different rates depending upon the amount of deposit, the interest rate, and the length of time money is left on deposit.

b. Have the students read the directions for Exercise 8.3, *Racing Toward a Goal*, in *Student Workouts*. Assign each student one of the eight situations. (Or make up teams of 8 students and have each student select a different situation.) Have each student complete the *Calculation Sheet* with *Racing Toward a Goal* to determine when his or her driver will meet the goal. Students could use calculators or a spreadsheet program to do the calculations.

c. When students have completed their calculations, they should compare their findings with their classmates' (or team's) findings to determine the correct order in which the drivers reached their goals. *(Answers are given on the next pages.)*

The correct order of racers is:

F H E G B C D A

(Completed calculation sheets for each racer are found below and on the next pages.)

Answer grid for $2,000 at 6% interest. Racer A reaches the goal of $40,000 in 13 years.

A	B	C	D	E	F	G
Year	Beginning Balance (from G)	Annual Deposit	New Balance (B+C)	Interest Rate	Interest Earned (D×E)	Total (D+F)
1	0	$2,000	$2,000	0.06	120.00	$2,120
2	$2,120.00	$2,000	$4,120.00	0.06	247.20	$4,367.20
3	$4,367.20	$2,000	$6,367.20	0.06	382.03	$6,749.23
4	$6,749.23	$2,000	$8,749.23	0.06	524.95	$9,274.19
5	$9,274.19	$2,000	$11,274.19	0.06	676.45	$11,950.64
6	$11,950.64	$2,000	$13,950.64	0.06	837.04	$14,787.68
7	$14,787.68	$2,000	$16,787.68	0.06	1007.26	$17,794.94
8	$17,794.94	$2,000	$19,794.94	0.06	1187.70	$20,982.64
9	$20,982.64	$2,000	$22,982.64	0.06	1378.96	$24,361.60
10	$24,361.60	$2,000	$26,361.60	0.06	1581.70	$27,943.30
11	$27,943.30	$2,000	$29,943.30	0.06	1796.60	$31,739.90
12	$31,739.90	$2,000	$33,739.90	0.06	2024.39	$35,764.29
13	$35,764.29	$2,000	$37,764.29	0.06	2265.86	$40,030.15

Answer grid for $2,000 at 10% interest. Racer B reaches the goal of $29,000 in 9 years.

A	B	C	D	E	F	G
Year	Beginning Balance (from G)	Annual Deposit	New Balance (B+C)	Interest Rate	Interest Earned (D×E)	Total (D+F)
1	0	$2,000	$2,000.00	10%	200.00	$2,200.00
2	$2,200.00	$2,000	$4,200.00	10%	420.00	$4,620.00
3	$4,620.00	$2,000	$6,620.00	10%	662.00	$7,282.00
4	$7,282.00	$2,000	$9,282.00	10%	928.20	$10,210.20
5	$10,210.20	$2,000	$12,210.20	10%	1221.02	$13,431.22
6	$13,431.22	$2,000	$15,431.22	10%	1543.12	$16,974.34
7	$16,974.34	$2,000	$18,974.34	10%	1897.43	$20,871.77
8	$20,871.77	$2,000	$22,871.77	10%	2287.18	$25,158.95
9	$25,158.95	$2,000	$27,158.95	10%	2715.90	$29,874.85

Answer grid for $3,000 at 6% interest. Racer C reaches the goal of $41,000 in 10 years.

A	B	C	D	E	F	G
Year	Beginning Balance (from G)	Annual Deposit	New Balance (B+C)	Interest Rate	Interest Earned (D×E)	Total (D+F)
1	0	$3,000	$3,000.00	0.06	$180.00	$3,180.00
2	$3,180.00	$3,000	$6,180.00	0.06	$370.80	$6,550.80
3	$6,550.80	$3,000	$9,550.80	0.06	$573.05	$10,123.85
4	$10,123.85	$3,000	$13,123.85	0.06	$787.43	$13,911.28
5	$13,911.28	$3,000	$16,911.28	0.06	$1,014.68	$17,925.96
6	$17,925.96	$3,000	$20,925.96	0.06	$1,255.56	$22,181.52
7	$22,181.52	$3,000	$25,181.52	0.06	$1,510.89	$26,692.41
8	$26,692.41	$3,000	$29,692.41	0.06	$1,781.54	$31,473.95
9	$31,473.95	$3,000	$34,473.95	0.06	$2,068.44	$36,542.39
10	$36,542.39	$3,000	$39,542.39	0.06	$2,372.54	$41,914.93

Answer grid for $3,000 at 10% interest. Racer D reaches the goal of $61,000 in 11 years.

A Year	B Beginning Balance (from G)	C Annual Deposit	D New Balance (B+C)	E Interest Rate	F Interest Earned (D×E)	G Total (D+F)
1	0	$3,000	$3,000.00	10%	300.00	$3,300.00
2	$3,300.00	$3,000	$6,300.00	10%	630.00	$6,930.00
3	$6,930.00	$3,000	$9,930.00	10%	993.00	$10,923.00
4	$10,923.00	$3,000	$13,923.00	10%	1,392.30	$15,315.30
5	$15,315.30	$3,000	$18,315.30	10%	1,831.53	$20,146.83
6	$20,146.83	$3,000	$23,146.83	10%	2,314.68	$25,461.51
7	$25,461.51	$3,000	$28,461.51	10%	2,846.15	$31,307.66
8	$31,307.66	$3,000	$34,307.66	10%	3,430.77	$37,738.43
9	$37,738.43	$3,000	$40,738.43	10%	4,073.84	$44,812.27
10	$44,812.27	$3,000	$47,812.27	10%	4,781.23	$52,593.50
11	$52,593.50	$3,000	$55,593.50	10%	5,559.35	$61,152.85

Answer grid for $4,000 at 6% interest. Racer E reaches the goal of $35,000 in 7 years.

A Year	B Beginning Balance (from G)	C Annual Deposit	D New Balance (B+C)	E Interest Rate	F Interest Earned (D×E)	G Total (D+F)
1	0	$4,000	$4,000.00	0.06	$240.00	$4,240.00
2	$4,240.00	$4,000	$8,240.00	0.06	$494.40	$8,734.40
3	$8,734.40	$4,000	$12,734.40	0.06	$764.06	$13,498.46
4	$13,498.46	$4,000	$17,498.46	0.06	$1,049.91	$18,548.37
5	$18,548.37	$4,000	$22,548.37	0.06	$1,352.90	$23,901.27
6	$23,901.27	$4,000	$27,901.27	0.06	$1,674.08	$29,575.35
7	$29,575.35	$4,000	$33,575.35	0.06	$2,014.52	$35,589.87

Answer grid for $4,000 at 10% interest. Racer F reaches the goal of $26,000 in 5 years.

A Year	B Beginning Balance (from G)	C Annual Deposit	D New Balance (B+C)	E Interest Rate	F Interest Earned (D×E)	G Total (D+F)
1	0	$4,000	$4,000.00	10%	$400.00	$4,400.00
2	$4,400.00	$4,000	$8,400.00	10%	$840.00	$9,240.00
3	$9,240.00	$4,000	$13,240.00	10%	$1,324.00	$14,564.00
4	$14,564.00	$4,000	$18,564.00	10%	$1,856.40	$20,420.40
5	$20,420.40	$4,000	$24,420.40	10%	$2,442.04	$26,862.44

Answer grid for $5,000 at 6% interest. Racer G reaches the goal of $52,000 in 8 years.

A Year	B Beginning Balance (from G)	C Annual Deposit	D New Balance (B+C)	E Interest Rate	F Interest Earned (D×E)	G Total (D+F)
1	0	$5,000	$5,000.00	0.06	$300.00	$5,300.00
2	$5,300.00	$5,000	$10,300.00	0.06	$618.00	$10,918.00
3	$10,918.00	$5,000	$15,918.00	0.06	$955.08	$16,873.08
4	$16,873.08	$5,000	$21,873.08	0.06	$1,312.38	$23,185.46
5	$23,185.46	$5,000	$28,185.46	0.06	$1,691.13	$29,876.59
6	$29,876.59	$5,000	$34,876.59	0.06	$2,092.60	$36,969.19
7	$36,969.19	$5,000	$41,969.19	0.06	$2,518.15	$44,487.34
8	$44,487.34	$5,000	$49,487.34	0.06	$2,969.24	$52,456.58

Financial Fitness for Life: Shaping Up Your Financial Future Teacher Guide, ©National Council on Economic Education

Answer grid for $5,000 at 10% interest. Racer H reaches the goal of $42,000 in 6 years.

A	B	C	D	E	F	G
Year	Beginning Balance (from G)	Annual Deposit	New Balance (B+C)	Interest Rate	Interest Earned (D×E)	Total (D+F)
1	O	$5,000	$5,000.00	10%	$500.00	$5,500.00
2	$5,500.00	$5,000	$10,500.00	10%	$1,050.00	$11,550.00
3	$11,550.00	$5,000	$16,550.00	10%	$1,655.00	$18,205.00
4	$18,205.00	$5,000	$23,205.00	10%	$2,320.50	$25,525.50
5	$25,525.50	$5,000	$30,525.50	10%	$3,052.55	$33,578.05
6	$33,578.05	$5,000	$38,578.05	10%	$3,857.81	$42,435.86

6. Explain that there is an easy way to estimate the extent to which interest compounds when it is left to accumulate. It is called the *Rule of 72*. The *Rule of 72* estimates how long it takes for money to double. Simply divide the number 72 by the interest rate, and the answer is the **approximate** number of years required to double your money. For example, at 10% interest, money doubles in about 7.2 years (72 ÷ 10 = 7.2); at 7% interest, money doubles in about 10.3 years (72 ÷ 7 = 10.3).

a. In Exercise 8.4, *Checking Out the Rule of 72: Does It Work?* students will be trying to find out if the Rule of 72 is accurate in predicting how long it will take for $100,000 to double at different interest rates.

b. Have the students use an on-line interest calculator such as the one found at **www.1728.com/compint.htm** to check out the Rule of 72.

c. They should use this procedure:
1. Solve for YEARS
  ▲ Input Principal: 100,000
  ▲ Input Total: 200,000
    (i.e. double the principal)
  ▲ Input Rate (do NOT use a decimal [e.g. 6% = 6])
2. Click on CALCULATE
  ▲ The answer will be the number of years it takes for the principal to double.

d. Ask: "Does the Rule of 72 work?"
(Students should observe that the Rule of 72 is fairly accurate in estimating the length of time for money to double. In each of the examples, money nearly doubles according to the Rule of 72.)

COOL DOWN

Ask the students the following questions:

1. What is simple interest? *(Interest earned on the principal and paid out to the depositor.)*

2. What is compound interest? *(Interest computed on the sum of the principal and previously earned interest.)*

3. What determines the amount of interest earned? *(The interest rate, the amount of the principal, and the length of time on which the interest is calculated.)*

4. If you left $3,000 in a savings account earning 8% interest, how many years would it take to double in size? *(Nine years, when estimated by the rule of 72, or 72 ÷ 8 = 9)*

Assessment

Have students complete Assessment 8.1 as a quiz or independent activity. Answers are shown on Answer key for Assessment 8.1, which follows the visuals for lesson 8.

Other Training Equipment

An annotated bibliography and additional Internet resources are available on our web site, **www.ncee.net**, as well as in *The Parents' Guide to Shaping Up Your Financial Future.*

Visual 8.1

Interesting Information about Interest

Interest
The price paid for using someone else's money.

Interest Rate
The price paid for using someone else's money, expressed as a percentage.

Principal
Basic amount deposited, **without** adding interest earned.

Simple Interest
Interest earned on the principal and **paid out** to a depositor.

Compound Interest
Interest computed on the sum of the principal **and** previously earned interest.

Compounding
The practice of leaving interest earned **on deposit**, so that it too earns interest.

Visual 8.2A

Simple Interest

A Deposit Cycle	B Beginning Balance (from previous G)	C Deposited Amount	D New Balance (B+C)	E Rate of Interest	F Interest Earned and paid out (D×E)	G Ending Balance (D)
1	0	10	10	20%	2	10
2		10		20%		
3		10		20%		
4		10		20%		
5		10		20%		
6		10		20%		
Total						

Financial Fitness for Life: Shaping Up Your Financial Future Teacher Guide, ©National Council on Economic Education

Visual 8.2B

Compound Interest

A	B	C	D	E	F	G
Deposit Cycle	Beginning Balance (from previous G)	Deposited Amount	New Balance (B+C)	Rate of Interest	Interest Earned and left in acct. (D×E)	Ending Balance (F+D)
1	0	10	10	20%	2	12
2		10		20%		
3		10		20%		
4		10		20%		
5		10		20%		
6		10		20%		
Total						

Round decimals to closest whole number.

Financial Fitness for Life: Shaping Up Your Financial Future Teacher Guide, ©National Council on Economic Education

Visual 8.3A

Simple Interest (Answers)

A Deposit Cycle	B Beginning Balance (from previous G)	C Deposited Amount	D New Balance (B+C)	E Rate of Interest	F Interest Earned and paid out (D×E)	G Ending Balance (D)
1	0	10	10	20%	2	10
2	10	10	20	20%	4	20
3	20	10	30	20%	6	30
4	30	10	40	20%	8	40
5	40	10	50	20%	10	50
6	50	10	60	20%	12	60
Total		60			42	

Visual 8.3B

Compound Interest (Answers)

A Deposit Cycle	B Beginning Balance (from previous G)	C Deposited Amount	D New Balance (B + C)	E Rate of Interest	F Interest Earned and left in acct. (D × E)	G Ending Balance (F + D)
1	0	10	10	20%	2	12
2	12	10	22	20%	4	26
3	26	10	36	20%	7	43
4	43	10	53	20%	11	64
5	64	10	74	20%	15	89
6	89	10	99	20%	20	119
Total		60			59	

Decimals have been rounded to the closest whole number.

Visual 8.4

Factors that Affect How Money Grows

Amount of money left on deposit

Interest Rate

Length of time money is left on deposit

ASSESSMENT

8.1 Answer Key

Factors that Affect How Money Grows*

Beginning values:
Amount.....................$5,000
Interest rate...................5%
Time..............................5 years

Change only the amount:
Amount.........................$10,000
Interest rate............................5%
Time....................................5 years

Change only the interest rate:
Amount.......................................$5,000
Interest rate..................................10%
Time...5 years

Change only the time:
Amount.............................$5,000
Interest rate...........................5%
Time..........................10 years

Year	Year Start Balance	Interest Rate	Interest Earned	Year End Balance
1	$5,000.00	5%	$250.00	$5,250.00
2	5,250.00	5%	262.50	5,512.50
3	5,512.50	5%	275.63	5,788.13
4	5,788.13	5%	289.41	6,077.54
5	6,077.54	5%	303.88	6,381.42
1	$10,000.00	5%	500.00	10,500.00
2	10,500.00	5%	525.00	11,025.00
3	11,025.00	5%	551.25	11,576.25
4	11,576.25	5%	578.81	12,155.06
5	12,155.06	5%	607.75	12,762.81
1	$5,000.00	10%	500.00	5,500.00
2	5,500.00	10%	550.00	6,050.00
3	6,050.00	10%	605.00	6,655.00
4	6,655.00	10%	665.50	7,320.50
5	7,320.50	10%	732.05	8,052.55
1	$5,000.00	5%	250.00	5,250.00
2	5,250.00	5%	262.50	5,512.50
3	5,512.50	5%	275.63	5,788.13
4	5,788.13	5%	289.41	6,077.54
5	6,077.54	5%	303.88	6,381.42
6	6,381.42	5%	319.07	6,700.49
7	6,700.49	5%	335.02	7,035.51
8	7,035.51	5%	351.78	7,387.29
9	7,387.29	5%	369.36	7,756.65
10	7,756.65	5%	387.83	8,144.48

If rounding of cents is not completed in each year, the answers will vary from the answer key.

81

THEME 3

LESSON

9

Stocks and Mutual Funds

Fitness Focus

EQUIPMENT
AND GETTING READY!

Make overhead transparencies of
the visuals listed here.

✔ Visual 9.1, **Steps in the Life
of a Stock**

✔ Visual 9.2, **The Secondary Markets**

✔ Introductory reading for Lesson 9
(**Shaping Up Your Financial Future
Student Workouts**)

✔ Exercise 9.1, **An Interview with Mr.
Stock (Shaping Up Your Financial
Future Student Workouts)**

✔ Exercise 9.2, **Juanita's
Decisions (Shaping Up Your
Financial Future Student
Workouts)**

✔ Six sheets of poster
board (one for each
group)

✔ Art supplies

✔ Magazines

LESSON DESCRIPTION AND BACKGROUND

In this lesson, the students examine the nature of stocks including how
stocks are issued, differences in their levels of risk, and the differences in
possible returns. The students also compare and contrast stocks with
various savings plans provided by financial institutions. The nature of
mutual funds, which allows diversification and reduction of risk, will also
be covered.

This lesson is correlated with national standards for mathematics and
economics as well as the national guidelines for personal financial management as shown in Tables 1 through 3 in the front of the book.

ECONOMIC AND PERSONAL
FINANCE CONCEPTS

Equity, stocks, mutual funds, risk, diversification

PARENT CONNECTION

There is no specific family activity for this lesson, but there are activities in *The Parents' Guide to Shaping Up Your Financial Future* that
parents may want to use with this lesson. These activities can be
found in the "Raising the Bar" section of Theme 3.

The Parents' Guide is a tool for reinforcing and extending
the instruction provided in the classroom. It includes:

1. Content background in the form of frequently
asked questions.

**TIME
REQUIRED
2 to 3
class periods**

82

2. Interesting activities that parents can do with their son or daughter.

3. An annotated listing of books and Internet resources related to each theme.

Workout

WARM-UP

1. Introduce the lesson by asking the students if they've heard of stocks. Ask the students to describe stocks. Ask them whether they can explain the differences between U.S. Savings Bonds and a stock. *(Bonds are debt instruments; stocks are equity.)*

2. Choose two students to role-play the interview with Mr. Stock, Exercise 9.1 in *Student Workouts*. After the role-play, discuss the answers to questions found in the exercise. Answers to questions are:

a. *Stocks show ownership or equity in a corporation.*

b. *Firms receive money from a stock when it is initially issued.*

c. *Stocks are primarily traded at stock exchanges (e. g. New York and American) and through brokerage houses that make a market in specific stocks (NASDAQ).*

d. *Advantages of owning stocks: owns part of business, has a voice in the business, has the possibility of getting above average return on investment. Disadvantages: may lose investment, may not receive any annual return.*

e. *Stock owners receive their return in two ways—dividends that they receive and selling their stocks for more than they paid for them.*

f. *U.S. Savings Bonds, corporate bonds, and other savings instruments are debt. This means that the party purchasing the bonds or putting money in a savings account is*

loaning money to another party for a period of time. Stockholders are owners of a corporation; they have a voice in the selection of people who run the corporation.

g. *With bonds, there is a promise that interest will be paid and that the loan will be repaid. Stockholders are not promised a return on their investment, or that the amount invested will be repaid if they sell the stock.*

h. *People buy stocks because they want the possibility of earning a greater return on their investment than is possible with other investments.*

3. Have the students read the *Warm-Up* for Lesson 9 in *Student Workouts*. Discuss the ideas presented in the reading with the class.

Student Objectives

At the end of this lesson, the student will be able to:

✔ Explain that stocks are ownership in a corporation.

✔ Explain the risk associated with stock ownership.

✔ Compare and contrast an investment in stocks with an investment in savings plans.

✔ Explain two ways in which stocks provide a return to owners.

✔ Differentiate between the primary and secondary markets for stocks.

✔ Define mutual funds and cite different types.

✔ Define diversification.

83

EXERCISE

1. How Stocks are Exchanged

a. Display Visual 9.1, *Steps in the Life of a Stock*, and explain that a stock is a share of ownership in a business, so stockholders are owners. Stocks are also called *equities*, meaning they are property. Each share owned by the stockholder entitles him or her to vote for the business's top managers or directors. In addition, each share entitles the stockholder to a share of the business's profits.

b. Using Visual 9.1 as a guide, describe how stocks are created and issued. When a business needs money to grow, it can issue stock. The first issue of the stock is called an *Initial Public Offering or IPO*. This big block of stock shares is sold to an investment firm that specializes in initial offerings of stocks. This sale takes place in the *primary market*. The primary market is where stocks are offered for sale the first time. The investment firm then sells smaller blocks to its best customers.

c. Display Visual 9.2, *Secondary Markets*, and explain that the *secondary market* is where stocks are bought and sold after the initial offering. The secondary market primarily consists of stock exchanges and over-the-counter markets. The major stock exchanges in the United States are the New York Stock Exchange and the American Stock Exchange. Stocks bought and sold on these exchanges are only those listed on the exchanges. NASDAQ is the major over-the counter market. In the NASDAQ market, individual brokerage houses *make markets* in specific stocks. Making a market means that the brokerage house is a centralized place where a certain stock can be traded. As a member of NASDAQ, the brokerage house reports the sales to a centralized location so that others will know what the stock is selling for at a particular time.

d. Redisplay Visual 9.1, *Life of a Stock*. Explain that when Success, Inc.'s shares of stock were purchased in the primary market, Success, Inc. got the money. But, Success, Inc. will never get money from the sale of its stock after its primary market sale. It no longer owns the stock. Ownership has been transferred to the purchaser of the stock. The next time those shares of stocks are sold, the money will go to the stockholder selling the stock.

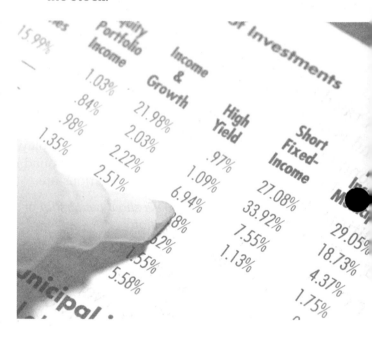

2. The Risks of Owning Stocks Compared to Loaning Money

a. Indicate that savings instruments and U.S. Savings Bonds are forms of debt. In the case of savings instruments, the person putting money into a savings account, a CD, or a money market deposit account are loaning money to the financial institution to loan out to other people. In the case of U.S. Savings Bonds, the person buying the bond is loaning money to the U. S. government. Corporations also issue bonds. They sell bonds, just like the government, which investors buy. Investors receive interest at least two times a year on the debt and there is a certain time when the corpora-

3. Mutual Funds

a. Explain that investors can reduce their risk by purchasing stocks in the form of mutual funds. Demonstrate mutual funds by placing a small box on your desk. Introduce yourself as the fund manager. Open a newspaper to the stock report page. Name a stock and say something like, "Hmm, IBM. I think I'll buy 10,000 shares of this." Cut a small chunk out of the paper and place it in the box. Continue doing this four or five times. Each time, mention a Blue Chip stock such as International Paper Company, Boeing Company, McDonalds, General Motors, Ford Motor Company, or Wal-Mart Stores, Inc.

b. Remind the students that you are the fund manager. This means you pick the stocks and the amount of shares of the stocks that will be included in the fund. As a fund manager, you want your fund to increase in value. By purchasing many different stocks, you reduce the risk that your fund will lose money because even if some stocks in your fund go down in value, it is likely other stocks in your fund will go up in value.

c. Explain that having many different stocks allows investors to reduce their risk. Having many different stocks, as well as other investment and some cash is called *diversification*. If an investor wants diversification, she or he can carefully choose many different stocks to include in his or her holdings. Or, she or he can buy shares in a mutual fund. If a person holds shares in a mutual fund, he or she is holding shares of stock in all of the companies included in the fund.

d. Place another small box on your desk. Go through the same procedure as above, but this time name smaller company stocks, such as Grey Wolf, Inc., Covad Communications Group, Inc., S3, Inc., and CenturyTel, Inc. Ask the students if they have detected any difference in these two mutual funds. (The students have likely not heard of these companies.)

tion must pay back the amount of the loan. After that background, have the students read the case problem in Exercise 9.2 and answer the three questions. The answers are:

1. *Creditors are favored over owners when firms are liquidated.*

2. *The stocks were riskier to Juanita since she did not receive any dividends or a return of her investment.*

3. *All stocks are not riskier than bonds. A stock in a company that is well run and has a good track record as to profitability carries less risk than a bond in a firm that is just getting started or is having difficulty making a profit. When looking at stocks and bonds issued by the same firm, though, stocks are riskier than bonds because of the differences in legal rights of stockholders and bondholders.*

b. Point out an important maxim in the investment world—the more risk of losing your money, the higher the possible return. Or the less risk, the lower the possible return. This has been very true of investments over the long run.

85

e. Explain that the first fund contained all "*blue chip*" stocks. These are stocks in big companies that have been doing a profitable business for a long time. It is not likely that the price of these stocks will decrease greatly. It is also unlikely that they will have large percentage increases in a short amount of time. This type of "blue-chip" mutual fund is considered to provide sustained but relatively slow growth. It is for people who want to receive a regular income from their investments, don't want to risk losing large amounts of money, and are satisfied with small, sustained gains in value.

f. Explain that the second fund contained smaller companies that look like they will prosper, but how well they will do in the future is uncertain. This is a *growth fund*, and it is riskier. It is for investors who are willing to lose some money but are hoping that these mid-size companies will grow and that the stock will increase greatly in value.

g. Point out that there are many different kinds of funds and that each carries different levels of risk. There are overseas growth funds containing stocks in foreign companies. There are money market funds that contain government-insured bonds. Each mutual fund is designed to meet the investment goals of a particular type of investor.

COOL DOWN

1. Have the students read the *Fitness Vocabulary*, *Muscle Developers*, and *Showing Your Strength* in *Student Workouts* as a review. Go over any of the concepts that they do not understand.

2. Remind the students that stocks offer an investor ownership in a company. As an owner, an investor faces the risk of losing part or all of his or her investment if the business fails. For that reason, an investor should purchase stock carefully. If he or she is comfortable with a relatively high level of risk, the investor may want to purchase stock in a small or new firm that shows great potential for growth. However, if an investor would rather have slow and steady growth, with less risk of losing his or her initial investment, stocks in stable, large companies would be preferred.

3. Ask the students what the following statement means, "Don't put all of your eggs in one basket." The students should recognize that if all of the eggs are in one basket and the basket falls, all of the eggs would be worthless. The same is true for investments. It is important that investors reduce their risk by having a number of diverse investment instruments. In part, this can be accomplished by choosing individual stocks carefully. However, this can also be accomplished by investing in mutual funds.

4. Ask the students the following questions:

a. What are stocks? (*Stocks are shares in the ownership of a business.*)

b. Why are stocks called equities? (*Equity means ownership, and stocks are ownership in a corporation.*)

c. What is the difference between stocks and bonds? (*Bonds are a debt of the issuer to the bondholder; stocks show ownership.*)

Financial Fitness for Life: Shaping Up Your Financial Future Teacher Guide, ©National Council on Economic Education

d. What is a primary market? *(It is the market where stocks are offered for the first time.)*

e. What are secondary markets? *(Secondary markets are those markets in which stocks can be bought or sold after being initially issued.)*

f. What are the risks associated with stock ownership? *(There is no guarantee of return on your investment. The price of the stock could go down or gain more slowly than other financial investments. The company could go bankrupt and the stockholder would likely lose his or her entire investment.)*

g. What are the returns for stocks? *(Dividends and capital gains.)*

Assessment

1. Explain that education offers many different areas of study. Students study math, history, language arts, science, and other subject areas. Ask the students to consider what their adult lives would be like if all they learned in school were math. Explain that there is diversity in the education they receive. Education provides an analogy for the importance of diversity in investments.

2. Place the students in six groups. Tell the students that they are to present an analogy of a diversified or undiversified stock portfolio in collage form or in a drawing. Be sure that students understand what an analogy is. *(A similarity between two things that can be compared.)*

Provide the students with poster board, magazines, and art supplies. Assign two groups each of the following topics: education, diet, and exercise. An "education poster" or drawing could depict a person's limited opportunities or abilities if he or she has studied only one subject area. A "diet" poster or collage could contain pictures of many types of foods representing a diversified diet that helps people remain healthy. An "exercise" poster or collage could include a depiction of what a person would look like if he or she only performed leg exercises at the gym.

3. Have each group make an oral presentation of their analogy as to why a diversified stock portfolio is important for financial health and well-being.

Other Training Equipment

An annotated bibliography and Internet resources can be found on our web site, **www.ncee.net**, and in *The Parents' Guide to Shaping Up Your Financial Future*.

Visual 9.1

Steps in the Life of a Stock

A stock can have a very long life. Stocks are little pieces of ownership in a corporation. As long as the corporation lives, so can its stocks. The following explains how a stock comes into existence and how the ownership of a company is traded among many people.

Success, Inc. needs money, so it sells one million shares of stock to

Money *Primary Market* New stocks

Morton Brothers, Inc. (an investment bank) which provides an **Initial Public Offering (IPO)** of shares of **Success, Inc.**

$ $ $

Secondary Market

Best Customer

Best Customer

Best Customer

The Best Customers can sell their shares of Success, Inc. stock to others through the **Secondary Market**

88

Visual 9.2

The Secondary Markets

Secondary markets are those markets in which stocks can be bought or sold after the initial public offering (IPO).

The major U.S. secondary markets are:

New York Stock Exchange (NYSE)

American Stock Exchange (AMEX)

NASDAQ

THEME 3

LESSON

10

Let Lenders and Borrowers Be

Fitness Focus

EQUIPMENT AND GETTING READY!

Make an overhead transparency of the visual listed here.

✔ Visual 10.1, *Everybody's Community Bank*

✔ Introductory reading for Lesson 10 (*Shaping Up Your Financial Future Student Workouts*)

✔ Exercise 10.1, *Calamity in Cow Town (Shaping Up Your Financial Future Student Workouts)*

✔ Reading 10.1, *Meet Me at the Stock Market (Shaping Up Your Financial Future Student Workouts)*

✔ Assessment Sheet 10.1, *Financial Terms (Shaping Up Your Financial Future Student Workouts)*

**TIME REQUIRED
1 to 2
class periods**

LESSON DESCRIPTION AND BACKGROUND

Financial intermediaries perform an important function in our economy. Financial institutions accept deposits from those who want both a safe haven for their funds and income from the use of their funds. These institutions also lend funds to people who want to borrow. Investment bankers and stockbrokers perform a similar function in that they bring together those who wish to sell equities with those who wish to invest. The managers of institutions, such as pension funds and mutual funds facilitate the transfer of money and investments. These are called *institutional investors*. In this lesson, the students learn the functions of financial intermediaries. They will recognize the benefits of successful transfers of funds and the opportunity costs of the decisions associated with the transfer of funds.

This lesson is correlated with national standards for mathematics and economics as well as the national guidelines for personal financial management as shown in Tables 1 through 3 in the front of the book.

ECONOMIC AND PERSONAL FINANCE CONCEPTS

Financial intermediaries, interest, opportunity cost, institutional investors, operating costs, profit

PARENT CONNECTION

There is no specific family activity for this lesson, but there are activities in *The Parents' Guide to Shaping Up Your Financial*

90

Future that parents may want to use with this lesson. These activities can be found in the "Raising the Bar" section of Theme 3.'

The Parents' Guide is a tool for reinforcing and extending the instruction provided in the classroom. It includes:

1. Content background in the form of frequently asked questions.

2. Interesting activities that parents can do with their son or daughter.

3. An annotated listing of books and Internet resources related to each theme.

Workout

WARM-UP

1. Remind the students that in a previous lesson they learned about several methods for saving money. All of the methods they learned about (savings accounts, certificates of deposit, money market deposit accounts, and U.S. Savings Bonds) are guaranteed in one way or another by the federal government. All of these savings methods are available through *financial intermediaries;* that is, institutions that transfer money from people who have saved money to people who want to borrow money.

2. Explain that the decisions of savers, bankers, and borrowers are affected by opportunity cost.

3. Define opportunity cost as the highest forgone alternative when a decision is made.

Student Objectives

At the end of this lesson, the student will be able to:

✔ Define and describe the different types of financial intermediaries.

✔ State that the price of money is interest and explain that the rate of interest is determined by supply and demand.

✔ State the functions of institutional investors operating in the stock market.

✔ State the opportunity cost incurred by savers, borrowers, stockholders, corporations issuing stocks, and banks.

EXERCISE

1. Everybody's Bank and Opportunity Cost

a. Display Visual 10.1. Explain that financial intermediaries, such as banks, credit unions, and savings and loan associations, are financial institutions that bring savers and borrowers together.

b. Direct the students' attention to *Everybody's Bank*. Savers deposit money in the bank to earn interest. The interest received must exceed the next

best alternative that they have for saving. For example, if savers could get six percent on their savings deposit elsewhere, many would move their savings. Everybody's Community Bank would have to pay at least six percent to attract and keep deposits.

c. Explain that Everybody's Bank is in business to make a profit for its owners. Profit is the payment to bank owners who have

91

many alternative uses for their money. As long as the expected profit of bank ownership is greater than the expected profit of the alternative uses, the owners will remain bank owners. Profits are gained from the revenues of the bank. The greatest share of the bank's revenue comes from interest paid by borrowers. The bank's costs include employees' wages, rent for office space, and other operating costs. These are the costs of doing business. Another cost is the interest payments the banks must make to those who have deposited money into the facility. Profits or losses are the difference between revenues and expenses.

d. Point out that borrowers try to borrow money at the lowest interest rate possible. They also experience opportunity cost in borrowing, which is giving up future income to pay back the loan and the interest.

e. Explain that borrowers pay interest to compensate lenders for the use of borrowed money. The bank charges interest to cover a portion of the bank's cost of doing business, and to partially compensate bank owners. Therefore, interest is the price of the loan.

f. Have the students read the *Warm-Up, Fitness Vocabulary, Muscle Developers*, and *Showing Your Strength* of Lesson 10 in *Student Workouts*. Discuss any of the concepts which are difficult for the students to understand.

g. Remind the class that in the *Workouts* materials for this lesson, they were asked to think of the bank or other financial intermediary as a supermarket where an exchange can be made. For instance, a producer wants to sell milk and a consumer wants to buy milk. The supermarket offers the producer and the consumer a place where that exchange can happen. As with the working of other markets, the price is established through the interaction of buyers and sellers. Tell the class that the next activity shows how that interaction occurs.

2. Calamity in Cow Town and the Cost of Credit

a. Direct the students to Exercise 10.1, *Calamity in Cow Town*. After the students have completed the questions, discuss the answers as follows.

1. The demand increased when people's taste for milk increased. One factor that can affect the demand for a product is a change in people's tastes and preferences.

2. The quantity of milk supplied stayed the same. The cows could only produce the same amount of milk and there wasn't enough time for farmers to adjust the size of their herds.

3. The price of milk went up because demand increased while supply stayed constant.

4. The price of these items most likely increased also. They were complements to the milk, meaning they were items that were bought along with the milk. When the demand of an item goes up, the demand for its complement also goes up. So when the demand for milk increased, the demand for bananas and pineapple juice also increased. Therefore, the price of bananas and pineapple juice increased.

5. *The farmers in the town would have liked to have increased their milk production because they could get a higher price for their milk. However, it would be difficult for them to increase their production without getting more cows, and that takes time.*

b. Explain that supply and demand of money through financial intermediaries determines the interest rate, which is the price of money. This is similar to how the supply and demand of milk through the grocery store determines the price of milk.

c. Explain that savers, who are the suppliers of funds, will be willing to save more money at higher interest rates and less money at lower interest rates. Remind the students that this is similar to farmers who would be willing to supply more milk at higher prices and less milk at lower prices. The farmer would take the money budgeted for savings, or spending for other items needed for the farm, and would spend the money to buy more cows. The opportunity cost would be the other things the farmer could have had with the money. In the same way, savers have other uses for their money. The interest rate must be high enough to encourage savers not to spend their money but to save it.

d. Point out that borrowers, on the other hand, are the demanders of funds. They will borrow less money at higher interest rates and more money at lower interest rates. Borrowers also have an opportunity cost. The higher the interest rate, the more things they will have to give up because of the higher interest.

e. Explain that, in general, the rate of interest paid to savers and paid by borrowers is determined in the marketplace by supply and demand. What savers provide in savings and what borrowers buy in the way of loans relates to how they view the opportunity cost of savings and borrowing at different prices (interest rates.)

3. Stocks

a. Explain that businesses are a major group seeking funds. From time to time, businesses need money to increase the size of operations. A business can borrow from banks, but it can also acquire money by selling a part of its ownership. In the same way that banks and other financial intermediaries bring savers and borrowers together, the investment banker brings the corporations (sellers of stock) and individuals or organizations (buyers of stock) together. The goals for the parties are the same. People who loan money or buy part of a company's ownership are doing so to earn income. Businesses that borrow or sell part of their ownership are trying to raise funds.

b. The stock market brings those who want to purchase shares of ownership together with those who want to sell shares of ownership. Remind the students that in the last lesson they learned about the stock market. Other kinds of financial intermediaries operate in the stock market. They are investment bankers and managers of brokerage firms, pension funds, and mutual funds.

c. Refer the students to Reading 10.1, *Meet Me at the Stock Market.* When the students have finished, discuss the reading by asking the following questions:

▲ **What are some examples of institutional investors?** *(Managers of brokerage firms, pension funds, mutual funds.)*

▲ **What is the goal of institutional investors?** *(To make money for their clients.)*

▲ **How do institutional investors decide which stocks to buy?** *(Institutional investors investigate companies to see which look financially sound and have good growth potential.)*

93

▲ **In what way do mutual funds, pension funds, and brokerage firms act as financial intermediaries?** *(They bring together people who wish to purchase ownership [their clients] with those who wish to sell ownership.)*

d. Explain that those who buy partial ownership in a corporation are called shareholders. Opportunity cost is as important to shareholders as it is to savers and borrowers. When institutions or individuals buy partial ownership in a company, they expect that the company will do well and earn a profit. As shareholders, they will share in part of the profit. A shareholder could use the money he or she spent on shares in the company to make other investments or to spend on goods and services.

e. Explain that corporations that sell partial ownership also experience opportunity cost. They give up shares of the ownership and the profit that those shares would have earned.

f. Explain that if a shareholder is not getting the expected return, he or she may sell the stock through the stock market to someone who is willing to buy it.

g. Ask the following questions:

▲ **Why would a company be willing to give up part ownership?** *(By selling shares of the ownership, a company raises money to expand business.)*

▲ **What is the opportunity cost incurred by someone who buys shares in a corporation?** *(Someone who buys shares gives up other investments or goods and services that could have been purchased with that money.)*

▲ **What can a shareholder do if he or she isn't earning the expected return?** *(The shareholder can sell the shares through the stock market.)*

COOL DOWN

Review the main concepts of the lesson by asking the following questions.

▲ **What are financial intermediaries?** *(Institutions that transfer funds to those who want them from those who have them.)*

▲ **What are some examples of financial intermediaries?** *(Banks, credit unions, savings & loan associations, pension funds, mutual funds, brokerage firms.)*

▲ **What is the price of money that is saved or borrowed?** *(Interest.)*

▲ **How is the rate of interest determined?** *(Supply and demand.)*

▲ **Why would savers want to be a part of the banking process?** *(Savers deposit savings in financial institutions that yield them a level of interest income exceeding the next best alternative for their savings.)*

▲ **Why would borrowers want to be a part of this process?** *(Borrowers can get money they want to make purchases and pay the money back over time.)*

▲ **Why would banks want to be a part of this process?** *(Banks earn income by facilitating exchange among those who wish to save and those who wish to borrow. Banks profit by making wise loans with their deposits.)*

▲ **Why are interest rates different for borrowers and savers?** *(A bank charges an interest rate to borrowers that is sufficient to cover its operating cost, its interest payments to savers, and provide a profit to bank owners.)*

▲ **What might happen if borrowers failed to repay debts and interest?** *(The bank would not be able to cover its costs, and it would fail.)*

94

▲ **What is the goal of an institutional investor?** *(Institutional investors want to make money for their clients.)*

▲ **How do businesses benefit from their involvement with institutional investors?**

(Businesses raise money by selling part of their ownership. Institutional investors bring those who want to buy ownership together with those who want to sell ownership.)

Assessment

Have the student complete assessment sheet 10.1 *Financial Terms* (*Shaping Up Your Financial Future Student Workouts*). The answers are as follows: *1. h; 2. d; 3. f; 4. b; 5. i; 6. c; 7. a; 8. g; 9. e.*

Other Training Equipment

An annotated bibliography and Internet resources can be found on our web site, **www.ncee.net**, and in *The Parents' Guide to Shaping Up Your Financial Future*.

Visual 10.1

Everybody's Bank

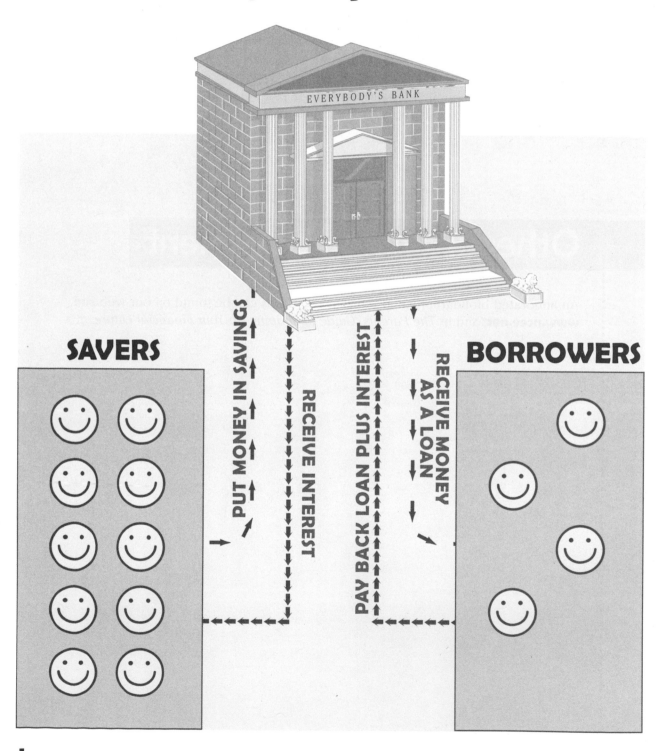

Financial Fitness for Life: Shaping Up Your Financial Future Teacher Guide, ©National Council on Economic Education

THEME 3

LESSON

11

Saving and Investing Are Risky Business

Fitness Focus

EQUIPMENT
AND GETTING READY!

Make an overhead transparency of the visual listed here.

✔ Visual 11.1, *Nothing is Risk-Free*

✔ Introductory reading for Lesson 11 *(Shaping Up Your Financial Future Student Workouts)*

✔ Exercise 7.1, *Types of Guaranteed Savings Instruments (Shaping Up Your Financial Future Student Workouts)*

✔ Exercise 11.1 *Now or Later? (Shaping Up Your Financial Future Student Workouts)*

✔ Exercise 11.2 *Decisions, Decisions (Shaping Up Your Financial Future Student Workouts)*

✔ Exercise 11.3 *Yield to the Investor (Shaping Up Your Financial Future Student Workouts)*

✔ Assessment 11.1, *Weighing All the Risks (Shaping Up Your Financial Future Student Workouts)*

✔ 103 pennies

✔ Calculators (one for each student)

✔ Newspaper or advertising pictures of items such as televisions, DVD player, car stereo system, clothing items, computer equipment.

✔ Internet access to sites, such as *www.money-rate.com* for the students to do extra credit work.

LESSON DESCRIPTION AND BACKGROUND

In this lesson, the students learn that savings and investment instruments carry various types of risk. Students learn about the risks of inflation, interest rate fluctuation, and financial loss. With any type of investment, there is at least one kind of risk. They also learn that risk must be measured against reward.

This lesson is correlated with national standards for mathematics and economics as well as the national guidelines for personal financial management as shown in Tables 1 through 3 in the front of the book.

ECONOMIC AND PERSONAL FINANCE CONCEPTS

Opportunity cost, inflation risk, interest rate risk, risk of financial loss, savings account, certificate of deposit, money market deposit account, U.S. savings bond

Student Objectives

At the end of this lesson, the student will be able to:

✔ Explain that all savings plans and investments carry risk.

✔ Match the types of risk with the savings plans and investments.

✔ State the opportunity cost associated with saving and investment.

97

PARENT CONNECTION

There is no specific family activity for this lesson, but there are activities in *The Parents' Guide to Shaping Up Your Financial Future* that parents may want to use with this lesson. These activities can be found in the "Raising the Bar" section for Theme 3.

The Parents' Guide is a tool for reinforcing and extending the instruction provided in the classroom. It includes:

1. Content background in the form of frequently asked questions.

2. Interesting activities that parents can do with their son or daughter.

3. An annotated listing of books and Internet resources related to each theme.

TIME REQUIRED 2 to 3 class periods

Workout

WARM-UP

1. Introduce the lesson by noting that one reason people use savings accounts is that they believe that savings accounts are risk-free. Explain that most banks and savings and loan associations carry insurance on their savings accounts through the Federal Deposit Insurance Corporation (FDIC). The FDIC insures an individual's accounts in one institution up to $100,000. In other words, if the bank or savings and loan closes and it is insured (most are), the depositors will get all their money back from the FDIC if they have $100,000 or less deposited in that bank. The same type of insurance is available from the National Credit Union Association (NCUA) for credit unions. The federal government guarantees the repay-ment of savings bonds, which provides about as much security as one can have in a savings plan.

2. Explain that the amount of the principal is secure with these plans. There is little risk of losing one's investment or principal. *Principal* is the amount of money placed in the account by the saver. Savers do not risk losing their savings; however, they do face other risks that are important to understand.

3. Have the students read the *Warm-Up*, *Fitness Vocabulary*, *Muscle Developers*, and *Showing Your Strength* for Lesson 11 in *Student Workouts*. Discuss the concepts that are difficult for the students.

EXERCISE

1. Inflation Risk

a. Invite a volunteer to the front of the class. Give the volunteer 100 pennies and explain that each penny represents $10. Ask the class how much money the volunteer has? *($1,000)* Explain to the volunteer that she or he could purchase a top-of-the-line stereo system for $1,000 but has decided to wait until next year to purchase the stereo system. He or she places the money in a regular savings account. Even though the interest rate on a regular savings account can fluctu-ate over time, explain that the interest rate did not change throughout the year and the volunteer received three percent interest on his or her $1,000. Ask how much the volunteer has after one year in his/her account? *($1,030)* You may have to review how interest is figured. The formula is:

**Interest =
Principal × Interest Rate × Time**
(Based on One Year)

Give the volunteer three more pennies.

b. Display Visual 11.1, *Nothing is Risk-Free*, and discuss inflation risk. This is the risk that the value of investments will not increase at least as rapidly as the rate of inflation. *Inflation* is a general rise in prices. When prices increase, your money is worth less and you lose buying power.

c. Explain to the class that the rate of inflation for the year was four percent. If the price of the stereo increased at the rate of inflation, the price of the stereo will now be priced at *$1,040 (1.04 × $1000)*. Ask the class if the volunteer has enough money to buy the stereo now. *(No, the saver is worse off now because he or she has lost purchasing power over the year.)* The student was guaranteed that she/he would not lose any of the money placed in the account and that interest would be gained, but inflation risk shows that the earned interest was not sufficient to maintain the purchasing power of the money. Have the student return to his/her seat.

d. Repeat that inflation is a general rise in the price level. This means that not all items increase in price, but on average prices have increased. Some items may not increase at the rate of inflation, while others will exceed this rate.

e. Refer the students to Exercise 11.1, *Now or Later?* in *Student Workouts* and, if possible, display pictures of the five items cut from store ads or magazines. The students will calculate the percentage change in the price of each item.

Discuss the questions on Exercise 11.1. The percentage change answers are listed in the table below. The amount in the account at the end of the year is $1,004.25. The answers to the questions follow:

1. *The computer and the camcorder.*
2. *None.*
3. *One year's wardrobe.*
4. *Computer.*
5. *The television, the car stereo system, and one year's wardrobe.*

f. Direct the students back to the description of certificates of deposits in Reading 7.1 (from Lesson 7 in *Student Workouts*). Explain that certificates of deposit (CDs) offer a higher interest rate than a statement savings account and a guarantee that the interest rate will stay the same throughout the period that the saver owns the CD. Suppose someone purchases a CD

Answers to Exercise 11.1, Now or Later?

Item	Last year's price	This year's price	% change
computer	$ 997.00	$ 897.30	−10
digital camcorder	$1,005.00	$ 954.75	−5
digital television	$1,000.00	$1,070.00	+7
car stereo system	$ 995.00	$1,074.60	+8
one year's wardrobe	$ 995.00	$1,094.50	+10

99

for $1,000 that pays six percent interest annually but must be held by the saver for two years. Ask the class to calculate the amount of interest the saver will get over two years. Explain that in this case, the bank will compound the interest annually, meaning it will award interest at the end of year one and then again at the end of year two. *($1,000×.06×1 = $1,060 after year one. $1,060×.06×1 = $1,123.60 after two years).*

g. Instruct the class to calculate how much the digital television, the price of which is $1,000 this year, would cost after two years at an annual inflation rate of four percent the first year and seven percent the second year. We are assuming that the television increases in price at the same rate as inflation. *($1,000×.04 = $1,040 after year one. $1,040×.07 = $1,112.80 after year two).* Ask if the saver would have enough money to buy the television if the money were kept in a CD. *(Yes.)* Explain that the saver retained more purchasing power because he or she gained over the inflation rate the first year. In this case, the purchasing power was maintained but the savings gained very little new purchasing power.

2. Interest Rate Risk

a. Point out a second type of risk, referring back to Visual 11.1. *Interest rate risk* is the risk that interest rates may change while the saver is "locked in" to a time deposit. This can be good for the saver if interest rates go down. If interest rates go up, the saver will "lose" the additional interest possible if the rate were not fixed.

b. Indicate that generally as inflation increases, interest rates increase. Notice in the last example that there was a four percent inflation rate one year and a seven percent inflation rate over the next year. During the first year, the CD paid over the inflation rate; in fact, it paid six percent. But during the last year, it did not keep up with inflation because it was locked in at a lower rate. Probably

the new CDs during that second year were yielding more than seven percent. So, during the last year, the money was not earning as much as it could because it was tied up in a savings plan where it could not be removed without penalty.

c. Use Exercise 7.1 to review the nature of the statement savings account, money market deposit account, and U. S. Savings Bond. Point out that the interest rate for the money market deposit account is flexible, as are the interest rates for U.S. Savings Bonds and for statement savings accounts. This is particularly advantageous in an inflationary time. As interest rates spiral upward in the market, these savings instruments also pay a higher rate.

3. **Summary Exercise**—Refer students to Exercise 11.2, *Decisions, Decisions*, in *Student Workouts*, and ask the students what they would do in the stated situations. The answers are:

a. *Statement savings account would be the best choice; the fact that interest rates may be decreasing is immaterial in this situation since you want the money readily available, and there is not enough savings for a CD or a money market deposit account.*

b. *Money market deposit account or statement savings account are the best choices. You have enough savings to secure a money market deposit account. You want to take advantage of the increasing rates.*

c. *Certificate of deposit of less than three years would be the best choice because you want to lock in the higher rate. You have enough savings to buy a CD.*

d. *U.S. Savings Bond would be the best choice; you have a small amount, so CDs and the money market are not available to you; savings bonds generally pay a better rate than statement savings accounts. They can also have a tax advantage, especially if used for education.*

Financial Fitness for Life: Shaping Up Your Financial Future Teacher Guide, ©National Council on Economic Education

e. *Money market deposit account or a state-ment savings account would be the best choice if the periodic withdrawals are unpredictable.*

4. Risk of Financial Loss

a. Ask if anyone has heard of the "Great Depression"? What happened during that time? Indicate that during that time many people went bankrupt because of their losses on the stock market. This points out a third type of risk, which is the financial risk, or risk of losing princi-pal (the amount invested or saved) or the return on the principal.

b. Show Visual 11.1, which defines the risk of loss as the possibility of losing the amount invested, or the principal.

c. Have the students look at Exercise 7.1 again and decide what the financial risk is for these savings plans. *(Students should indicate that there is very little risk of loss of principal if a savings bank fails because FDIC insurance protects against loss for savings accounts, certificates of deposits, and money market deposit funds. The United States Government stands behind the repayment of U.S. Savings Bonds. There is a risk of some financial loss for CDs and U.S. Savings Bonds if they are cashed prior to the maturity date.)*

d. Ask students why stocks carry substan-tially more risk of principal loss than the savings plans? *(Stocks show ownership in a corporation; there is no insurance or guarantee from the government that the firm will make a profit or be successful.)*

5. Rate of Return: A Way to Compare Investments

a. Indicate that in a market economy, there is a general principle that investments with greater risk have the possibility of a greater return. In order to compare the returns from different saving or investment choices, one must know how to figure the rate of return. The rate of

return is based on the percentage return an investment has made during the year.

c. Show students how to determine the annual return from a savings account.

$$\frac{\textbf{Amount of Interest}}{\textbf{Amount Invested}} \times 100 = \textbf{percent}$$

Suppose that Sue received $50 on her savings account. The amount that she had in her savings account at the beginning of the year was $1,000. She did not put any additional deposits into the account.

$$\frac{\$50}{\$1,000} = .05$$

$$.05 \times 100 = 5\%$$

d. Indicate that the return for stock is based on two figures—dividends and capital gains or losses. The *capital gains or losses* are the difference between the purchase price and the market price at the end of the year. Technically, capital gains or loss-es are figured only when a stock has been sold. For purposes of figuring the rate of return for the year, one must use the end of the year figure. For example, if some-one pays $40 for a stock and at the end of the year the stock is selling at $50 the capital gain (if sold) would be $10. If the stock were selling at $30, the capital loss would be $10 per share.

Financial Fitness for Life: Shaping Up Your Financial Future Teacher Guide, ©National Council on Economic Education

The formula for figuring the rate of return on an investment for a stock is as follows:

Dividend During Year
$$\frac{\textbf{+ Capital Gain or Loss}}{\textbf{Amount Invested}} \times \textbf{100} = \textbf{\%}$$

Suppose that Justin bought 100 shares of stock at $30 per share at the beginning of the year. The stock paid $2 in dividends per share during the year, and is selling at $31/share at the end of the year. What is the estimated rate of return if one sold the stock at the end of the year?

$$\frac{(\$2 \times 100) + (\$1.00 \times 100)}{\frac{\$200 + \$100}{\$3,000}} \times 100 = 10\%$$

Distribute Exercise 11.3, *Yield to the Investor*, that asks students to determine the rate of return on various types of investments and savings plans. The answers are as follows:

1. *3%*
2. *10%*
3. *12%*
4. *2%*
5. *Number three has the best return. Stockholders are entitled to a better return than what is gained from a savings account because they assume more risk in owning stocks.*

COOL DOWN

Remind the students that each type of savings or investment instrument carries risk. Review these types of risk by asking the following questions:

▲ **Describe inflation risk.** *(This is the risk that the value of investments will not increase at least as rapidly as the rate of inflation.)*

▲ **What types of savings instruments that we have studied would carry inflation risk?** *(All savings instruments carry inflation risk.)*

▲ **Describe interest rate risk.** *(This is the risk that interest rates may change while the saver is "locked in" to a deposit for a period of time.)*

▲ **What types of savings instruments that we have studied would carry higher interest rate risk?** *(Certificates of deposit.)*

▲ **Describe risk of financial loss.** *(This is the risk of losing principal, the amount of money invested.)*

▲ **Do stocks or bonds generally carry a greater risk of financial loss?** *(Stocks.)*

102

Assessment

**Have student complete Assessment 11.1,
Weighing All the Risks, in Student
Workouts. The answers are:**

1. *Savings accounts carry an inflation rate risk.
Even though the rate increases with the general increase in interest rate, the low rate on
these accounts may not keep up with inflation.*

2. *Primary risks for a certificate of deposit (CD)
are interest rate risk and inflation risk. These
may be a problem if inflation and interest
rates increase during the time of the CD pur-*

*chasing power decreases. On the other hand,
a CD can be beneficial if inflation and interest rates decline during the time interval
because the rate is locked in.*

3. *Primary risk is inflation risk, since the interest rate offered for savings bonds may not be
much higher than the inflation rate. There is
a financial risk (losing interest earned) if
you cash it in early.*

4. *Risk of financial loss is the major risk of
stock investments.*

Other Training Equipment

An annotated bibliography and Internet resources can be found on our web site,
www.ncee.net, and in *The Parents' Guide to Shaping Up Your Financial Future.*

Visual 11.1

Nothing is Risk-Free

Inflation risk: Risk that the value of investments will not increase at least as rapidly as the rate of inflation.

Interest rate risk: Risk that interest rates may change while the saver is "locked in" to a time deposit.

Financial Risk: Risk of losing principal (the amount of money invested), and the return on the principal.

THEME 4

LESSON

12

Cash or Credit?

Fitness Focus

EQUIPMENT
AND GETTING READY!

Make overhead transparencies of the visuals listed here.

✔ Visual 12.1, *Advantages and Disadvantages of Various Methods of Payment*

✔ Visual 12.2, *How a Check Works*

✔ Visual 12.3, *How a Credit Card Works*

✔ Introductory reading for Theme 4 and Lesson 12 *(Shaping Up Your Financial Future Student Workouts)*

✔ Exercise 12.1, *So Many Credit Card Offers: What's the Difference? (Shaping Up Your Financial Future Student Workouts)*

✔ Exercise 12.2, *Cash or Credit? You Be the Judge (Shaping Up Your Financial Future Student Workouts)*

✔ Exercise 12.3, *Understanding a Credit Card Statement (Shaping Up Your Financial Future Student Workouts)*

✔ Assessment 12.1, *Rubric for Evaluating Panel Discussion (Shaping Up Your Financial Future Student Workouts)*

✔ Family Activity 7, *Credit Card Coin Toss (The Parents' Guide to Shaping Up Your Financial Future)*

✔ Credit Card Application Forms—one for each student. You will need to collect these ahead of time, or have students bring in those their parents receive.

LESSON DESCRIPTION AND BACKGROUND

Most students are aware of the variety of spending options available to consumers. Cash, checks, debit cards, and credit cards are often used by their parents; however, the students probably do not understand the implications of each. This lesson examines the advantages and disadvantages of various payment methods and focuses especially on credit usage. The students are challenged to calculate the cost of credit, compare credit card agreements, and analyze case studies to determine whether credit is being used wisely. In the Family Activity, the students and their families will examine the extent of credit and debt in the United States economy and participate in a game comparing credit card criteria.

This lesson is correlated with national standards for mathematics and economics as well as the national guidelines for personal financial management as shown in Tables 1 through 3 in the front of the book.

ECONOMIC AND PERSONAL FINANCE CONCEPTS

Interest, interest rate, credit, opportunity cost, inflation.

Student Objectives

At the end of this lesson, the student will be able to:

✔ Differentiate between forms of cash payment and credit.

✔ Compare the advantages and disadvantages of using credit.

✔ Explain how interest is calculated.

✔ Analyze the opportunity cost of using credit and various forms of cash payments.

✔ Evaluate the costs and benefits of various credit card agreements.

105

PARENT CONNECTION

Refer to Family Activity 7, *Credit Card Coin Toss* in *The Parents' Guide to Shaping Up Your Financial Future*. Ask the students to complete the activity at home and encourage them to share with their families what they have learned about the advantages and disadvantages of using credit.

The Parents' Guide is a tool for reinforcing and extending the instruction provided in the classroom. It includes:

1. Content background in the form of frequently asked questions.

2. Interesting activities that parents can do with their son or daughter.

3. An annotated listing of books and Internet resources related to each theme.

Workout

WARM-UP

1. Introduce the lesson by asking the students to name some different ways people can pay for goods and services. Guide their responses to make sure that credit is one of them. *(Possible responses should include cash, check, debit card, gift certificate, credit card.)* Write their suggestions on Visual 12.1.

2. Ask students to suggest advantages and disadvantages of each payment method, and write their ideas on the overhead transparency. *(Suggested answers in the table on next page.)*

3. Explain that cash, checks, or debit cards are forms of money. They can be used as a medium of exchange in most transactions.

4. Explain that credit is not money, but is actually a loan. When a person uses a credit card, his or her signature on the credit receipt verifies an agreement to pay back the money at a later date, with interest if not paid by a certain time.

5. Display Visual 12.2, *How a Check Works,* and Visual 12.3, *How a Credit Card Works.* Discuss the processes, making sure the students

understand that a check is drawn on an existing account, and credit is an I.O.U.—a loan—that must be repaid, usually with interest.

6. Review the concept of opportunity cost, the next best alternative that is given up when a choice is made. Ask what Chad's opportunity

	Advantages	**Disadvantages**
Currency (Paper money)	Fast, no paperwork, acceptable.	Can be stolen, lost; might not have enough. Cannot be used for telephone or Internet purchases.
Coins	Fast, no paperwork, acceptable.	Heavy, can be stolen or lost, only small purchases. Cannot be used for telephone or Internet purchases.
Check	Safe, good for different amounts.	Might not be accepted, need identification, must record each check amount, limited by amount in checking account. Cannot be used for telephone or Internet purchases.
Gift Certificate	Just like currency.	Only good at specific store, sometimes need identification. May have expiration date.
Debit Card	Safe, confidential, no need for cash.	Must record each purchase amount, limited by amount in checking account. Need to remember PIN. May not be accepted.
Credit	Safe, not responsible for all purchases made on stolen card. Can be used for telephone or Internet purchases.	Must pay interest; may incur fees if balance not paid by due date. May not be accepted.

cost was when he spent $50 at the music shop and paid with a check. (*He gave up the opportunity to earn interest on the $50 or to buy something else with the $50, which ever would have been his next best choice.*)

7. Ask what Chad's opportunity cost was when he bought the video game and used his credit card. (*His opportunity cost lies in the future. He will have to give up the opportunity to buy something else with the $50 he has to pay back when the credit card bill is due.*)

8. Have the students read the *Introduction* to Theme 4 and the *Warm-Up, Fitness Vocabulary, Muscle Development* and *Showing Your Strength* for Lesson 12 in *Student Workouts.* Discuss the new vocabulary, and make sure the students understand the concepts.

EXERCISE

1. Choosing a Credit Card

a. Display a number of credit card applications that you have clearly marked "VOID" and from which you have deleted any personal information. Review the relevant vocabulary (annual fee, annual percentage rate, grace period, interest rate, minimum payment.)

b. Distribute one application to each student, and have the students work in pairs, using their two applications to complete Exercise 12.1, *So Many Credit Card Offers: What's the*

Difference? in *Student Workouts. (Answers will vary, but students should note that they need to analyze all aspects of an offer, i.e. interest rate, grace period, minimum payment, etc. before deciding which offer is best..)*

c. Explain that choosing a credit card should be like choosing any other goods or services. People should shop around and compare different credit cards before making a decision.

d. Explain that credit offers consumers the opportunity to enjoy a product while they are paying for it. Another good thing about credit is that it allows a consumer to take advantage of sales to buy goods or services at a lower price when the consumer does not have enough money.

e. Distribute calculators to the students and review the math processes required to calculate interest. (If some of the students are proficient with spreadsheets, you may wish to have them construct a spreadsheet to complete this activity.)

f. Have the students work in pairs to complete Exercise 12.2, *Cash or Credit? You Be the Judge* in *Student Workouts.* Answers follow:

1. *Elizabeth—Because of inflation the stereo will cost $1,030; Elizabeth will save $1,080; she will be able to buy the stereo and will have $50 plus interest earned over the year left over.*

2. *David—Will pay back the $800 in one month; he will pay no interest.*

3. *Ryan—It will take Ryan 10 months to pay off his credit card debt; he will have spent $851.47 including interest. The calculations are shown below.*

4. *Caitlin—Paying only the minimum monthly payment, it will take Caitlin almost 15 years to pay her credit card debt, and she will have paid $2,034.04, which includes interest of $1,234.04.*

g. Ask the students to compare the choices of the four consumers and decide who made the best decision. *(David's choice appears to be best. David got the enjoyment of his stereo right away, and because he paid his credit card balance in full, he paid no interest. Elizabeth had to wait a year to begin enjoying her stereo, and because of inflation, her cost was $1,030. Ryan got the enjoyment of the stereo while he made his monthly payments, but his total cost was $851.47. Caitlin got to enjoy her stereo right away, but it took her about 15 years to pay for it, and the total*

Answers to 3. Ryan's Credit Card Summary

A	B	C	D	E	F	G
No. of Months	Amount Owed (Col. G on line before)	Amount paid each month	New Balance (B – C)	Annual Interest @ 18% (D x .18)	New Monthly Interest (E ÷ 12)	Amount Owed (D + F)
Month 1	$800.00	90.00	710.00	127.80	10.65	720.65
2	720.65	90.00	630.65	113.52	9.46	640.11
3	640.11	90.00	550.11	99.02	8.25	558.36
4	558.36	90.00	468.36	84.31	7.03	475.39
5	475.39	90.00	385.39	69.37	5.78	391.17
6	391.17	90.00	301.17	54.21	4.52	305.69
7	305.69	90.00	215.69	38.82	3.24	218.93
8	218.93	90.00	128.93	23.21	1.93	130.86
9	130.86	90.00	40.86	7.36	0.61	41.47
10	41.47	41.47	0.00			
	Total Paid	851.47			51.47	

Financial Fitness for Life: Shaping Up Your Financial Future Teacher Guide, ©National Council on Economic Education

cost was more than $2,000. Students may comment that Caitlin will undoubtedly want a newer and better stereo before she finished paying for the present one.)

2. Reading a Credit Card Statement

a. Explain that when people make credit card purchases, they receive a monthly credit card statement that contains information about their purchases, payments and fees.

b. Have the students examine the sample credit card statement in Exercise 12.3, *Understanding a Credit Card Statement*, in *Student Workouts*. Discuss the various components, making sure the students understand the following:

1. **Total credit line**—The maximum amount that can be charged.

2. **Total available credit**—Total credit line minus the new balance.

3. **Cash limit**—Maximum amount that can be used for a cash advance.

4. **Cash available**—Cash limit minus new balance.

5. **Amount past due**—Any amount that was not paid on time.

6. **Statement closing date**—The date of the last purchase billed on this statement.

7. **New balance**—What is now owed.

8. **Payment due date**—Date by which the minimum payment must be made.

9. **Minimum payment**—The least amount that must be paid to avoid penalty.

10. **Previous balance**—Last month's balance.

11. **Payments**—How much was paid in the last billing period.

12. **Other credits**—Any refunds posted to the account in the last billing period.

13. **Purchases**—Total amount spent in this billing cycle; this is itemized in another part of the statement.

14. **Cash advances**—Amount charged to this account for cash received.

15. **Other fees**—Late fees or other service charges.

16. **Finance charge**—Interest incurred on previous balance.

17. **Grace period**—Time when no interest is charged on new purchases if the new balance is paid in full by the payment due date.

c. Demonstrate how the new balance was computed. See Box.

Previous balance	**$345.55**
Minus payments	**−200.00**
	145.55
Plus Purchases	207.64
Plus late fee	29.00
Plus finance charge	5.30
New Balance	**$387.49**

d. Have the students complete Exercise 12.3 as an independent assignment. (Answers:)

1. *February 10, 2001.*

2. *December 20, 2000.*

3. *Fee for late payment.*

4. *The credit limit is $3,000.*

5. *$207.64*

6. *$200.00*

7. *$3,000.00*

8. *$2,612.00*

9. *$5.30*

10. *Because he or she did not pay the balance in full last month.*

11. *Answers will vary, but it appears that the consumer is paying a major portion of his or her credit card debt but has had difficulty in making the monthly payments on time ($29 late fee).*

COOL DOWN

1. Have the students collect credit card applications from their families for about two weeks or until the class has approximately 20 applications. Clearly mark "VOID" on each page, and delete or obscure any personal information. Then, using a long roll of white or butcher paper, have the students construct a grid like the one below, to compare the credit cards according to the following criteria: annual fee, grace period, interest rate, credit limit.

Name of Card					
Issuing Bank					
Annual Fee					
Grace Period					
Interest Rate					
Credit Limit					

2. When the grid is complete, engage the students in a discussion of the costs and benefits of each card. Remind the students that the use of credit involves an opportunity cost in the future.

Assessment

As an assessment measure, have the students work in groups of three or four to prepare a panel discussion that addresses the use of credit. Use Assessment 12.1 Answer Key to evaluate the students' panel discussion.

Other Training Equipment

An annotated list of books and Internet resources that relate to this topic are available on our web site, **www.ncee.net**, as well as in *The Parents' Guide to Shaping Up Your Financial Future.*

Visual 12.1

Advantages and Disadvantages of Various Methods of Payment

Payment Option	Advantages	Disadvantages

Visual 12.2

How a Check Works

1. Chad writes a $50 check to pay for music CDs.

2. The shop owner sends Chad's check to her bank (A).

3. Bank A processes Chad's check and sends it to Chad's bank (B).

4. Bank B deducts $50 from Chad's checking account, and electronically notifies Bank A of the transaction.

5. Bank A electronically adds $50 to the shop owner's account.

6. Bank B sends Chad his cancelled check (or copy) for his records.

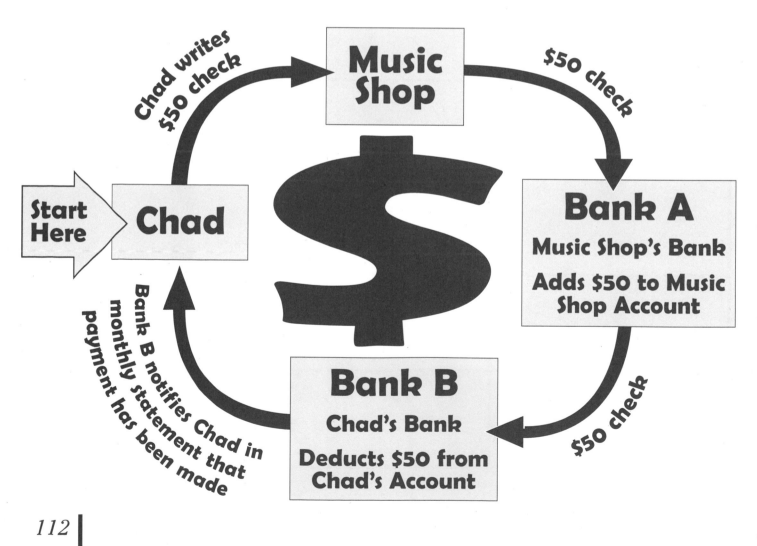

Financial Fitness for Life: Shaping Up Your Financial Future Teacher Guide, ©National Council on Economic Education

Visual 12.3

How a Credit Card Works

▲ Chad uses a credit card issued by ABC Credit Card Company to purchase video games.

▲ The store owner swipes Chad's credit card past a scanner.

▲ ABC Credit Card Company is quickly notified that Chad has requested $50 worth of credit, and if ABC Credit Card Company approves the charge, a credit sale occurs. The credit card company would add the amount of the item purchased to the store's account less a processing fee. The processing fee would go to the account of the store's merchant processor.

▲ ABC Credit Card Company sends Chad a statement that includes a record of his $50 purchase at the video store.

▲ If Chad pays the $50 before the due date, he usually won't have to pay any interest.

▲ If Chad chooses to pay only part of the $50, he will be charged interest on the remaining balance.

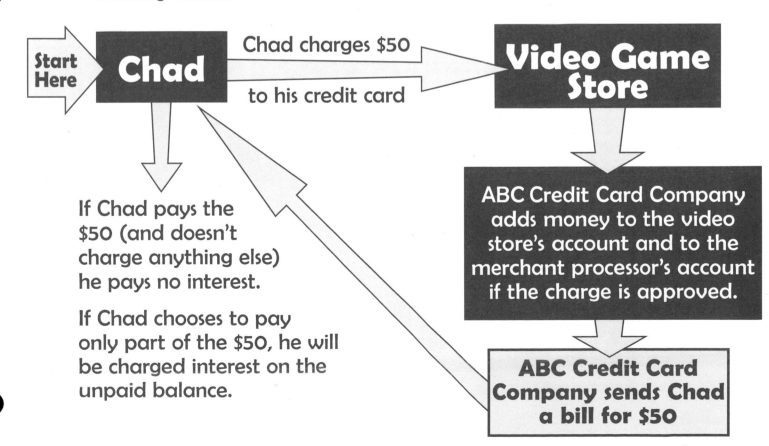

Start Here → **Chad**

Chad charges $50 to his credit card →

Video Game Store

If Chad pays the $50 (and doesn't charge anything else) he pays no interest.

If Chad chooses to pay only part of the $50, he will be charged interest on the unpaid balance.

ABC Credit Card Company adds money to the video store's account and to the merchant processor's account if the charge is approved.

ABC Credit Card Company sends Chad a bill for $50

ASSESSMENT

12.1
Answer
Key

Rubric for Evaluating Panel Discussion

Topics to be covered in Panel Discussion	Discussed thoroughly and accurately 2 points	Briefly discussed with some inaccuracies 1 point	Not discussed 0 points
Advantages of using credit			
Disadvantages of using credit			
APR			
Grace period			
Annual fees			
Transaction fees (late fees)			
Minimum payment and total cost			
Interesting statistics re credit			
Recommendations for wise credit use			
How inflation may affect decisions re use of credit			
The opportunity cost of credit			
Totals			
Grand Total of Three Columns			

THEME 4

LESSON

13

Establishing Credit

Fitness Focus

EQUIPMENT AND GETTING READY!

✔ Introductory reading for Lesson 13 *(Shaping Up Your Financial Future Student Workouts)*

✔ Reading 13.1, *Character Counts— So Do Capacity and Collateral (Shaping Up Your Financial Future Student Workouts)*

✔ Exercise 13.1 A, B, C and D, *Completed Loan Applications and Credit Reports for Applicant 1, 2, 3, and 4 (Shaping Up Your Financial Future Student Workouts)*

✔ Exercise 13.1E, *Applicant Summary Sheet (Shaping Up Your Financial Future Student Workouts)*

✔ Assessment 13.1, *Using Your Evaluation Skills (Shaping Up Your Financial Future Student Workouts)*

TIME REQUIRED
2
class periods

LESSON DESCRIPTION AND BACKGROUND

Lenders are in business to grant loans to individuals and businesses. However, the applicant's ability to repay a loan can mean the difference between profit and loss for the lender. To reduce risk, the lender assesses the applicant's credit-worthiness by reviewing his or her character, capacity for repayment, and collateral. In this lesson, the students will work through exercises to assess the three "Cs" of several loan applications. They will discover ways they can establish a credit record, and they will learn the rights and responsibilities they have as borrowers.

This lesson is correlated with national standards for mathematics and economics as well as the national guidelines for personal financial management as shown in Tables 1 through 3 in the front of the book.

ECONOMIC AND PERSONAL FINANCE CONCEPTS

The three "Cs" of credit, character, capacity, collateral, the rights and responsibilities of borrowers

Student Objectives

At the end of this lesson, the student will be able to:

✔ Define the three "Cs" of credit.

✔ Explain borrowers' rights when obtaining credit.

✔ Explain borrowers' responsibilities when managing credit.

✔ Describe ways a young person may establish credit.

115

There is no specific family activity for this lesson, but there are activities in *The Parents' Guide to Shaping Up Your Financial Future* that parents may want to use with this lesson. These activities can be found in the "Raising the Bar" section for Theme 4.

The Parents' Guide is a tool for reinforcing and extending the instruction provided in the classroom. It includes:

1. Content background in the form of frequently asked questions.

2. Interesting activities that parents can do with their son or daughter.

3. An annotated listing of books and Internet resources related to each theme.

Workout

WARM-UP

1. Have the students read the *Warm-Up, Fitness Vocabulary*, *Muscle Developers*, and *Showing Your Strength* for Lesson 13 in *Student Workouts*. Discuss the concepts in the readings.

2. Introduce the lesson by explaining that credit is a service. Sellers and credit-granting organizations, such as banks, provide consumers with credit. *Credit* is a loan extended to consumers.

3. Explain that those who provide credit for consumers are called *lenders*. Lenders must use caution when granting credit, so they look for certain characteristics among those

who apply for credit. These characteristics are referred to as the three "Cs" of credit. Direct the students' attention to Reading 13.1, *Character Counts—So Do Capacity and Collateral* in *Student Workouts*. After the students have finished the reading, review with the students what a lender looks for when evaluating the character, capacity, and collateral of a loan applicant.

EXERCISE

1. Evaluating a Loan Application

a. Break the students into six groups and assign Exercise 13.1A to two groups, Exercise 13.1B to two groups, and Exercise 13.1C to two groups.

b. Point out that the applications and credit reports shown in the students' exercise are not as lengthy as an actual loan application and credit report, but that the information provided on the exercise sheets will give the students enough information to make a decision. Help the students with any terminology they may not understand.

c. Refer the students to Exercise 13.1E, *Applicant Summary Sheet*. Instruct the students to use this exercise sheet to record their evaluation of the character, capacity, and collateral of the applicant. When each group has completed the task, a spokesperson from each group will present the group's assessment of the 3Cs, and whether they think a bank would approve the loan. Points that should be noted are covered in the following:

Exercise 13.1 Answers

1. THE ANDERSONS

Character: Pay rent and credit payments on time.

Capacity: Required payments for rent and credit payments are $1,089 per month (includes loan being applied for). Take home pay is $1,833. Couple should be able to afford payments.

Collateral: Good, considering their income. Have $5,000 cash.

Recommendation: Approve loan.

2. JOEY DELIGH

Character: Has problems making required payments.

Capacity: Required payments for rent and credit card payments are $2,386 per month (includes loan being applied for, excludes auto loan about to be paid in full). Net income is $2,667. Very little left for other expenses.

Collateral: Cash plus investments and equity in home is less than outstanding debt.

Recommendation: Would not approve loan unless the father meets lending criteria and is willing to co-sign loan.

3. THE RANSDIAS

Character: Good record of paying debt.

Capacity: Required payments for rent and credit payments are $4,696 per month (includes loan being applied for). Net income is $7,083. Have sufficient earnings to pay bills.

Collateral: Have more in collateral than loans.

Recommendation: Approve loan.

2. Rights and Responsibilities

a. Ask the students what they would do if they were denied a loan. *(The students may suggest that they would just do without the item they wished to purchase with the loan, that they would seek another source for a loan, or that they may seek information as to why they were denied the loan and take action to repair their credit report. All of these answers are acceptable.)*

b. Explain that borrowers have rights and responsibilities associated with the credit they obtain. When a person's application is denied, the applicant has a right to view his or her credit report free-of-charge within 30 days of denial. If the information on the report is in error, the credit reporting agency must change the information and notify lenders about the correction. If the applicant and the credit reporting agency do not agree with information on the report, the applicant has a right to attach his or her explanation of the problem to the credit report. This explanation must also be sent to lenders. These rights for credit consumers are guaranteed by the Fair Credit Reporting Act. Explain that there are other rights, including the right to :

1. Information about the Annual Percentage Rate and the total finance charges.

2. Eligibility for credit without discrimination based on sex, religion, nationality, or marital status.

3. Contest charges on your credit card statement if you think they are wrong.

4. Protection from abuse by credit collection agencies if you are late making payments.

c. Explain that along with these rights come responsibilities. Ask students what some responsibilities may be. *(Accept answers such as repayment of the loan plus interest, making payments on time, giving honest information on credit applications.)*

3. Establishing Credit

a. Ask the students if it would be easy or difficult for them to get credit approved. *(Difficult. They [as a rule] have no income, collateral, or history.)*

b. Have the students reread the first page of Reading 13.1 and then discuss ways that a person can develop a good credit history.

117

COOL DOWN

Review the "Cs" of credit and the rights and responsibilities of the borrower by asking the following questions.

▲ **When the lender is considering your character, what does he or she examine?** *(Your record of paying your credit debts on time; your history of managing finances, such as a checking account; your employment stability; and your residential stability.)*

▲ **When the lender is considering your capacity, what characteristics does he or she examine?** *(Your income from all sources, your current debts, and your net worth [the difference between everything you own and everything you owe to others.])*

▲ **Lenders want to be sure you don't just walk away from the loan without paying. They want to be sure you have collateral. What types of things would serve as collateral?** *(A car, a house, cash.)*

▲ **If you have no credit history, what could you do to establish credit?** *(Open a checking or savings account, establish a department store account or a layaway plan, obtain a small starter loan or credit card, get a co-signer for a loan.)*

▲ **What rights do you have as a borrower?** *(You cannot be discriminated against for gender or marital status; interest rates and fees must be disclosed to the borrower; you cannot be subject to abusive credit collection practices.)*

▲ **What are your responsibilities as a borrower?** *(The borrower must make, at least, the minimum payment when due; the borrower agrees to pay the finance charge; the borrower agrees to pay late fees for late payments.)*

Assessment

Assign students the Assessment 13.1, *Using Your Evaluation Skills*, in *Student Workouts*. Instruct the students to evaluate the application. *(Answers for evaluating Rhett Willis: Character: Sometimes has difficulty making payments on time, especially in the last six months. Always makes payments, though. Capacity: Required payments for rent, child support, and other outstanding debts are $1,728 [includes loan being applied for]. Net income per month is $2,504. Collateral: Savings and checking are more than credit card debt. Auto and motor home also count as collateral. Would recommend.)*

Other Training Equipment

An annotated bibliography and Internet resource list are available on our web site, **www.ncee.net**, and in *The Parents' Guide to Shaping Up Your Financial Future.*

THEME 4

LESSON

14

Comparison Shopping

Fitness Focus

EQUIPMENT AND GETTING READY!

Make overhead transparencies of the visuals listed here.

✔ Visual 14.1, *Major Steps in a Purchase Decision*

✔ Visual 14.2, *Decision-Making Grid for DVD Player*

All the exercises, readings, and the assessment are found in *Shaping Up Your Financial Future Student Workouts*

✔ Introductory reading for Lesson 14

✔ Exercise 14.1, *A Wise Person Once Said...*

✔ Exercise 14.2, *Major Steps in a Purchase Decision*

✔ Exercise 14.3, *Poor Mrs. Amos*

✔ Exercise 14.4, *The Worm Has Turned*

✔ Reading 14.1, *Comparison Shopping*

✔ Reading 14.2, *Liar, Liar, Pants on Fire*

✔ Assessment 14.1, *Major Steps in a Purchase Decision*

✔ Store advertisements and newspaper ads for the following consumer products: home audio entertainment system, home computer system, living room furnishings, used car, television, roller blades with helmet or pads (teacher may substitute other consumer products.)

LESSON DESCRIPTION AND BACKGROUND

For some people, shopping is an art, and they spend hours and hours making a purchase decision. For others, the goal is to get in, buy it, and get out! Neither of these approaches is necessarily efficient. Making correct consumer choices requires a plan of action—one that neither takes too much of the consumer's time nor places the consumer in a vulnerable, misinformed position. In this lesson, the students learn a seven-step approach to making a well-informed consumption decision. They also learn to avoid consumer mistakes.

This lesson is correlated with national standards for mathematics and economics as well as the national guidelines for personal financial management as shown in Tables 1 through 3 in the front of the book.

ECONOMIC AND PERSONAL FINANCE CONCEPTS

Comparison shopping, consumer protection

Student Objectives

At the end of this lesson, the student will be able to:

✔ State the seven steps in a purchase-making decision.

✔ Explain why each step is important.

✔ Make a purchase decision using the seven steps and the decision-making grid.

✔ Describe three illegal or deceptive practices found in the marketplace.

✔ Name the advantages and disadvantages of comparison shopping.

✔ Name at least two not-for-profit or government agencies who will help the consumer.

119

PARENT CONNECTION

There is no specific family activity for this lesson, but there are activities in *The Parents' Guide to Shaping Up Your Financial Future* that parents may want to use with this lesson. These activities can be found in the "Raising the Bar" section for Theme 4.

The Parents' Guide is a tool for reinforcing and extending the instruction provided in the classroom. It includes:

1. Content background in the form of frequently asked questions.

2. Interesting activities that parents can do with their son or daughter.

3. An annotated listing of books and Internet resources related to each theme.

TIME REQUIRED 2 to 3 class periods

Workout

WARM-UP

1. Introduce the lesson by explaining that people often make financial mistakes through haste and ignorance. This particularly applies to purchasing decisions. Refer the students to Exercise 14.1, *A Wise Person Once Said…* in *Student Workouts* and ask them to explain the two adages. Be sure the students understand the first statement by mentioning that "pound" refers to the United Kingdom pound sterling (the U.K. currency) and not a pound in weight. Then instruct them to contrast the two statements.

2. Call on the students to give their perceptions of the two statements. Explain that the first statement refers to people who make an effort to save a penny, but do so in ways that cost them later. For example, they buy a low-quality product, and it falls apart. The statement could also refer to people who seem to be careful with small purchases but careless with large purchases. The second statement suggests that people should be careful with even their smallest purchases, because every amount of money saved is like receiving that amount in income. Together, the statements reflect the thought that it is best to be careful about all purchases, no matter what the size.

3. Discuss with students what they think it means to "live within your means." Accept student answers; then explain that this statement recommends that people take care to limit their expenditures to their amount of income. Although this is good advice, even better advice would be to suggest people "live beneath their means." Ask the students to give examples of what it may mean to live beneath one's means. *(Answers will vary, but the students might suggest that although someone might be able to afford to buy a car with a $300 per month payment, they may be better off finding a car that requires only a $250 per month payment. In that way, the buyer has $50 each month to apply to savings.)*

4. Advise the students that living beneath your means doesn't necessarily mean doing without the things you want. Staying within a budget or even well below a level of income can be accomplished by comparison shopping.

EXERCISE

1. Comparison Shopping

a. Have the students read the *Warm-Up*, *Fitness Vocabulary*, *Muscle Developers*, and *Showing Your Strength* of Lesson 14 in *Student Workouts*.

b. Define comparison shopping and ask students if any of them comparison shop for the things that they buy. Ask why they comparison shop or do not comparison shop.

c. Refer the students to Reading 14.1, *Comparison Shopping*, in *Student Workouts*. Spend some time talking about the advantages and disadvantages of comparison shopping. Have students comment on how the following statement relates to the advantages and disadvantages of comparison shopping.

> **"Comparison shopping is more important for expensive, complex products than for inexpensive, simple products."**

d. Ask how the principle of opportunity costs relates to making decisions regarding comparison shopping. *(Comparison shopping takes time and money that could be used for something else. Sometimes, comparison shopping for inexpensive things means giving up something that is worth more to the individual than the benefits gained. Many times, however, the gain from careful shopping is worth more than the time and money given up.)*

e. Inform the students that they will have an opportunity to demonstrate their ability to get value for their money. However, there is a strategy involved in successful comparison shopping of which they should become aware. Display Visual 14.1, *The Major Steps in a Purchase Decision*, and discuss the steps as follows.

▲ **Identify what you want.** This may seem obvious, but writing down exactly what you want helps you avoid the impulse to buy things on the spur of the moment or to buy something that is low on your list of priorities.

▲ **Determine how much you can spend.** You know how much money you have to cover all of your purchases. So, determine how much you can spend and stick to your decision. It's very easy to rationalize spending only a few dollars more than you intended to.

However, if you do this with every item you purchase, you will eventually have to do without something you want when the money runs out.

▲ **Find out what products or services are available in your price range.** Determine the price range you can afford to pay and look at the options in that price range. Don't look at the more expensive options that are out of your price range, since you may be tempted to buy an item you cannot afford.

121

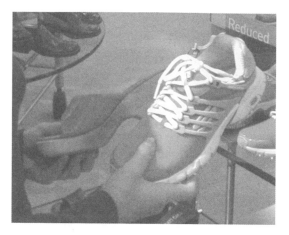

▲ **Choose the features you would most like to have.** List all the features in the product you want to buy so that you can compare each of the products in your price range.

▲ **Analyze the products in your price range to see if they have the features that you want.** The use of a decision-making grid helps in this analysis. Project Visual 14.2, *Decision-Making Grid for DVD Player*, which shows a completed decision-making grid for someone considering the purchase of a DVD Player. The steps in completing the grid are as follows:

1. List the alternatives along the side of the left-most column—in this case it is the various brands of the DVD Player.

2. List the features that you want along the top of the grid—these included remote control, surround audio system, and wide screen format option.

3. If a product has the feature, place a "+" in the appropriate cell. If the product does not have the feature, place a "–" in the appropriate cell.

4. Tally up the pluses to determine which would be the best choice from the analysis. In the example, the RCA DVD Player met all of the features, whereas the others did not. We also assume all the criteria have equal weight.

▲ **Watch for hidden costs.** Before making a final choice, look for any hidden costs associated with any of the alternatives you are considering, especially the one that is most attractive to you. These costs might include delivery costs, special taxes or surcharges, required accessories, or club membership. High hidden costs may encourage you to select a product other than your first choice.

▲ **Make your choice.** Decide on what you want, and stick to your decision. After using the good or service, determine whether it was a wise choice.

f. Invite the students to practice comparison shopping. Place the students in groups of three or four. Assign each team one of the following products or services. Have the students choose the store or newspaper ads featuring their consumer item.

▲ Home audio entertainment system ($300 budget)

▲ Home computer system ($1,000 budget)

▲ Living room furniture for a new apartment ($500 budget)

▲ Used car (($3,000 budget)

▲ Television set ($200 budget)

▲ Roller blades with helmet and pads ($200 budget)

g. Direct the students to use Exercise 14.2, *Major Steps in a Purchase Decision*, which includes a decision-making grid, to analyze the various options and make a decision.

h. To gather information about the product that they have been assigned, have them read the advertising that you have supplied, and/or have them comparison shop on the Internet or in the local community.

i. When the students have completed their assigned decision making, have them present their choices and how they arrived at their choices orally to the class.

2. Hindrances to Good Decision Making

a. Explain that even carefully made purchasing decisions can fail to satisfy the consumer. This happens for various reasons. Sometimes the consumer has not been fully informed. Sometimes the consumer can be made to feel pressured into a decision.

b. Choose three students to perform the role-play in Exercise 14.3, *Poor Mrs. Amos*, in *Student Workouts*. Instruct the students to pay particular attention to the tactics used by the salesman. When the students have completed the role-play, discuss the questions which are found on the exercise. Possible answers include:

1. *The salesman intimidated Mrs. Amos by comparing her yard to her neighbors' yards. He told her many of her peers use the lawn service. He minimized the cost of the service.*

2. *If Mrs. Amos was uncomfortable with his tactics, she should simply have hung up the phone.*

3. *Mrs. Amos continued to stay on the phone because she was polite; she did not want to appear rude; she was trusting.*

c. Explain to the students that each state has an office of the Attorney General. This office often receives complaints about illegal or unethical sales tactics. These tactics can be used against any of us.

d. Explain that the cost of a lawn service may be a relatively small item, but often the items offered by telephone sales people are large and costly. Many people have been "talked out of" very large amounts of money to buy everything from land to securities to insurance policies. This practice isn't limited to telephone sales, however. Consumers can walk into a sales office to buy cars, large appliances, or vacation homes and become just as intimidated.

e. Choose four students for the role-play Exercise 14.4, *The Worm Has Turned*, in *Student Workouts*. The four students will play the following parts: Mr. Allen, Tina Allen, the salesman, and the sales manager. The sales manager has no speaking part. Place the salesman, Mr. Allen, and Tina Allen, around a desk. Place the sales manager in a corner of the room. Instruct the sales manager and the salesman to pantomime an argument in the corner when the script·calls for the salesman to meet with the sales manager.

f. When the role-play is complete, discuss the questions which were on the exercise sheet. Possible answers include:

1. *The salesman tried to ingratiate himself with Tina and her father by asking Tina if she had just received her license; he discussed his own teenagers; he kept telling Tina and her father how much he liked them; he told them he would go to the manager on their behalf.*

2. *The salesman tried to pressure Tina and her dad by indicating that there was another customer coming in to buy the car.*

3. *Answers will vary, but students will probably think Tina was going to succumb to the pressure.*

4. *Tina did the right thing. Tina and her dad had a budgeted amount for the car, and they stuck to that budget.*

g. Explain that the Allens would do well to consult the newspaper, a web site, and the *Blue Book* to determine what cars fall into their price range. Then they can go to the dealership armed with good information.

h. Warn the students that there are other types of consumer pitfalls they should avoid. Refer the students to Reading 14.2, *Liar, Liar, Pants on Fire*. Engage the students in a discussion of examples of these practices they may have observed. Share your own experiences with the students.

i. Explain that there are many federal, state, and local laws that protect consumers. There are also not-for-profit organizations consumers can consult before buying a product or when they are having problems with a product already purchased.

123

Tell the students that they can find web sites for consumers by searching on "consumer protection." Explain that the students can protect themselves in the following ways.

▲ Ask your friends about their experiences with the store or sales office.

▲ Before making a purchase, consult the Better Business Bureau. You can call or visit it on-line at **www.bbb.org**. The BBB keeps lists of consumer complaints against stores and sales offices. The BBB works with the consumer and the stores or sales offices to clear the complaint. They can offer you information BEFORE you buy.

▲ Your state's Attorney General's office accepts consumer complaints. They will work with the consumer and the store or sales office to rectify complaints. They may also prosecute unscrupulous stores and sales offices.

▲ The Federal Trade Commission (**www.ftc.gov**) maintains federal laws protecting consumers. This is a federal agency acting in the interest of our citizens.

▲ The National Consumers League maintains a web site reporting incidents of telephone and Internet fraud. This site is located at **www.fraud.org**.

COOL DOWN

Explain that the students have learned about comparison shopping as well as how to protect themselves in the marketplace. Ask the following questions.

1. The first step in a purchase decision is to identify what you want. **Why is this step so important?** *(It forces you to define exactly what you want. By defining your wants, you avoid impulse buying.)*

2. The second step in a purchase decision is to determine how much you can spend. **Why is this step so important?** *(By setting a firm budget for the item, you can avoid being lured into a larger than expected expenditure. If you spend more than your budget will allow, you will have to give up something else you wanted.)*

3. The third step in a purchase decision is to find out what products or services are available in your price range. **Why is this step so important?** *(In order to be a well-informed consumer and get exactly what you want, you have to seek out every option available to you.)*

4. The fourth step in a purchase decision is to choose the features you would like to have. **Why is this step so important?** *(This helps you make comparisons among products and increases the likelihood that you will be happy with your purchase decision.)*

5. The fifth step is to analyze the alternatives according to the features that you want, using a decision-making grid. **Why is it important to analyze the alternatives?** *(To determine which is the best choice for you according to the features you want.)*

6. The sixth step in a purchase decision is to watch for hidden costs. **Why is this step so important?** *(You don't want the final cost of your purchase to exceed your budget.)*

Financial Fitness for Life: Shaping Up Your Financial Future Teacher Guide, ©National Council on Economic Education

7. How would you describe "bait and switch?" *(This is an illegal practice where the consumer is lured into the store to purchase a bargain-priced product only to be told the product is "sold out" and then referred to a pricier item.)*

8. What example can you give of deceptive pricing? *(Stores may offer a "special value" hoping to persuade the consumer that this is a reduced price when it actually is not.)*

9. What example can you give of deceptive advertising? *(Answers will vary.)*

10. If you are considering a purchase, how can you know you are dealing with a reputable store or sales office? *(Ask other people about their experiences with the store or sales office. Consult the Better Business Bureau or other consumer advocacy organization in your community.)*

Assessment

Assign the students the Assessment 14.1 in *Student Workouts*. Instruct them to choose a small item (under $75) they would like to purchase and follow the procedures they learned in this lesson. Answers will vary according to the good or service selected, and the criteria used to evaluate the alternatives.

Other Training Equipment

An annotated bibliography and Internet resources are available on our web-site **www.ncee.net**, as well as in *The Parents' Guide to Shaping Up Your Financial Future*.

125

Visual 14.1

Major Steps in a Purchase Decision

1. Identify what you want.

▲ Set your priorities.   ▲ Avoid impulse buying.

2. Determine how much you can or want to spend.

▲ Develop a budget and stick to it.

3. Find out what products or services are available in your price range.

▲ Check store ads.   ▲ Consult consumer magazines.

▲ Ask your friends.   ▲ Visit on-line vendors.

4. Choose the features you would most like to have.

▲ List specific characteristics/features the product/service must have and would be nice to have (optional).

▲ List the characteristics/features you definitely do not want.

5. Use the decision-making grid to analyze the alternatives.

▲ Use ⊕ for alternatives that have a feature, ⊖ for alternatives without the feature.

▲ Tally the plusses to determine best choice.

6. Watch for hidden costs.

▲ Check the sales tax. (Sales tax varies by community.)

▲ Check for delivery costs or costs of required accessories.

7. Make your choice.

Financial Fitness for Life: Shaping Up Your Financial Future Teacher Guide, ©National Council on Economic Education

Visual 14.2

Decision-making Grid for a DVD Player

Features ➡️ ⬇️ Alternatives	Feature 1 Remote Control	Feature 2 Surround Sound System	Feature 3 Wide Screen Format Option	Total Points
Item 1 Samsung	+	–	–	1
Item 2 Hitachi	+	+	–	2
Item 3 RCA	+	+	+	3
Item 4 Zenith	+	+	–	2

THEME 5

LESSON

15

Managing Cash

Fitness Focus

Make overhead transparencies of the visuals listed here.

✔ Visual 15.1, *Ways to Categorize Expenses*

✔ Visual 15.2, *Living Within Their Means (Answer Key)*

✔ Introductory reading for Theme 5 and Lesson 15 *(Shaping Up Your Financial Future Student Workouts)*

✔ Exercise 15.1, *Keeping Track of Cash Flow (Shaping Up Your Financial Future Student Workouts)*

✔ Exercise 15.2, *Living Within Their Means (Shaping Up Your Financial Future Student Workouts)*

✔ Parent Activity 8, *The Battle of the Budget Game (The Parents' Guide to Shaping Up Your Financial Future)*

✔ Assessment 15.1, *Tomorrow Never Budgets (Shaping Up Your Financial Future Student Workouts)*

✔ Calculators

LESSON DESCRIPTION AND BACKGROUND

Although most middle school and junior high students do not hold full-time jobs, they do have spending power. They may earn money from an allowance or a part-time job, and they have discretionary income that totals, by some estimates, billions of dollars a year.

Yet, while most teens are prolific consumers, most do not have a plan, or budget, for sensible spending and saving. This lesson will challenge the students to create a reasonable budget based on an appropriate allocation of income in a number of categories, such as clothing, entertainment, food, etc.

This lesson is correlated with national standards for mathematics and economics as well as the national guidelines for personal financial management as shown in Tables 1 through 3 in the front of the book.

ECONOMIC AND PERSONAL FINANCE CONCEPTS

Fixed expenses, variable expenses, periodic income, budget, opportunity cost, trade-off, planned expense, unplanned expense

Student Objectives

At the end of this lesson, the student will be able to:

✔ Distinguish between fixed and variable expenses as well as planned and unplanned expenses.

✔ Record and analyze one's expenses.

✔ Develop a budget.

✔ Evaluate how well a budget is kept based on expenses and income for a period.

PARENT CONNECTION

Family Activity 8 in *The Parents' Guide to Shaping Up Your Financial Future* asks the students to analyze the budgets of two feuding families, the Hatfields and the McCoys. Students are also asked to make recommendations about modifying the budgets when changes occur in income or expenses. Answers to this family activity are found in *The Parents' Guide*.

The Parents' Guide is a tool for reinforcing and extending the instruction provided in the classroom. It includes:

1. Content background in the form of frequently asked questions.

2. Interesting activities that parents can do with their son or daughter.

3. An annotated listing of books and Internet resources related to each theme.

Workout

WARM-UP

1. Introduce the lesson by asking the students to name important events that families and friends celebrate together. Make a list on the board as the students suggest events. *(Answers will vary; the students will probably name birthdays, weddings, family reunions, anniversaries, graduations, holidays and religious events.)*

2. Ask the students how families plan for each event: list their ideas next to the events on the board. *(Answers will vary; the students will probably suggest decorations, food, gifts, seating arrangements, entertainment, etc.)*

3. Engage the students in a discussion of how planning is important to the success of any event.

EXERCISE

1. Explain that planning is important in money matters, too. For example:

▲ **How does someone get enough money for a down payment for an automobile or home?** *(Planned saving.)*

▲ **How does a person make sure there is enough money for the entire month?** *(Plan spending carefully for the whole month.)*

2. Have the students read the *Warm-Up, Fitness Vocabulary, Muscle Developers*, and *Showing Your Muscle* for Lesson 15 in

Student Workouts. Discuss the ideas and review the new vocabulary, making sure the students understand the terminology.

3. Keeping Track of Cash Flow.

a. Explain that managing cash requires the students to examine how they earn money and how they spend it. A cash flow statement is one way of recording how money is spent—what they purchase, the amount, and whether the expense is planned or unplanned.

b. Show Visual 15.1 *Ways to Categorize Expenses*. Discuss *fixed* versus *variable expenses*, and *planned* versus *unplanned expenses*. Ask the students which expenses are more easily changed by the consumer (*variable*). Note that planned expenses include both variable and fixed expenses. Ask the students to think of some examples to add to each of the categories. (*Answers will vary.*)

c. Have the students turn to Exercise 15.1, *Keeping Track of Cash Flow*, and review the form with the students, noting the categories for food, clothing, entertainment, or other. Ask the students to keep track of their expenditures for one week on this form. Point out the sample line on the form where the expenditure is named (item/service) and the cost is listed in the *food* column. Each item is further marked as *fixed* or *variable* and whether it was a *planned* or *unplanned* purchase.

d. Emphasize the importance of recording *every* expenditure, no matter how small, and explain that when the students choose to spend money for one item, their opportunity cost is the next best alternative they could have bought instead.

e. At the end of the week, have the students total their expenditures (using calculators or paper and pencil) and record the totals for each category (food, clothing, entertainment, or other) on Exercise 15.1. Then have them total all expenditures for a *Grand Total*. Have the students recalculate the totals by adding all the planned expenses together, and all the unplanned expenses together. Students can also calculate how much they spend on fixed and variable expenses.

f. Have the students calculate the percentage of the grand total for each category. Explain how to calculate percentages. (Divide each expense by *Total Expenses* and then multiply by 100, e.g.:

▲ Amount spent for *Food* ÷ *Total Expenses* × 100 = % spent for *Food*.)

g. Discuss the answers to the questions in the exercise. (*Answers will vary. Students should note that variable expenses are the easiest to decrease.*)

h. Have the students develop a budget for the next week and record their expenses as before. At the end of the week, ask the students to evaluate how well they stayed within their budgets. Discuss what changes they could make to improve their budget for the next week.

5. Living Within Their Means.

a. Explain that financial advisors often examine the income and expense statements of individuals in order to determine whether their spending habits are reasonable. Divide the class into groups of four or five students and assign each group to read one case study from Exercise 15.2. After totaling the expenses and comparing them to monthly income, have each group answer questions 1-4. Then have each group report their answers to the class. (*Calculations are shown in the answer grid on Visual 15.2. Answers to questions 1-4 will vary.*)

b. Have students complete questions 5-9 which compares the budgets to one another. Discuss the answers. (The answers are: *(1) Lauren; (2) Brian, Maria, and Suzanne; (3) Lauren; (4) $68.33. (5)*

Answers will vary, but students might suggest that Lauren reduce her entertainment, phone, clothes, charity or savings to come up with $500.)

COOL DOWN

1. Divide the class into three groups and have them assume these roles:

▲ those who receive the same salary each week—e.g., from an allowance;

▲ those who receive a regular allowance plus periodic income—e.g., from occasional jobs;

▲ those who have only periodic income— e.g., no regular allowance, only occasional jobs such as baby sitting, mowing lawns, etc.

2. Each group should answer the questions below from the point of view of their group's type of worker.

▲ How do you estimate your income?

▲ How do you estimate your expenses?

▲ What is the hardest part about setting up your budget?

▲ How do fixed and variable expenses affect your budget?

▲ How do you handle emergencies that cause increases in expenses?

▲ Why do you pay yourself first?

▲ What budget advice would you give to people who have the same type of income sources that you do?

Assessment

Have the students complete Assessment 15.1 as an independent assignment. *(Answers are given below.)*

▲ *James Bond's expenses are less than his income; he has $538.00 left over. His total income is $1,974,654. His total expenses are $1,974,116.*

▲ *Answers may vary, but the students should respond that his opportunity cost is the next best alternative use of $175,000 that he must give up in order to buy the new plane. Perhaps he'll have to give up the maintenance of his home in Hawaii.*

▲ *Fifteen percent of Bond's income is $296,198.10, so he'll have to increase his current savings plan to follow the recommendation of his financial advisor. Bond's trade-off might be that he'll have to spend less on a number of other things, such as airplane tickets, restaurant meals, etc.*

131

Other Training Equipment

An annotated bibliography and Internet resource list are available on our web site, **www.ncee.net**, or in *The Parents' Guide to Shaping Up Your Financial Future.*

Visual 15.1

Ways to Categorize Expenses

FIXED EXPENSES
Spending that remains the same month to month.
▲ Rent or mortgage payment
▲ Car payment

VARIABLE EXPENSES
Spending that changes month to month.
▲ Long distance telephone bill
▲ Gas for the car
▲ Food purchased at restaurants
▲ Video rental

PLANNED EXPENSES
Spending you expect and for which you plan.
▲ Gift for your mother's birthday
▲ Friday night movie and ice cream
▲ Deposit to college savings account

UNPLANNED EXPENSES
Spending for an unexpected emergency, an urgent need, or an impulse purchase.
▲ Car repair for fender-bender
▲ Doctor visit for sprained ankle (or broken bone.)
▲ Fabulous sale at local music store
▲ Donation to collection for victims of earthquake

Visual 15.2

Living Within Their Means
Answer Grid

	Lauren	Brian	Maria	Suzanne	Marcus	Jeff
Annual income	$43,000	$35,000	$37,000	$130,000	$67,000	$28,950
Monthly income	$3,583.33	$2,916.67	$3,083.33	$10,833.33	$5,583.33	$2,412.50
Savings	$200	$185	$100	$1,485	$650	$200
Rent/Home	650	725	575	4,005	1,275	750
Utilities	300	240	285	550	285	65
Phone/cable/internet	150	175	225	275	95	45
Food/Groceries	225	207	375	275	275	95
Car payment	550	365	125	750	350	155
Insurance	156	148	220	625	215	115
Transportation	77	88	47	375	85	115
Charity	80	89	20	550	95	55
Clothes	55	115	185	225	150	40
Loan payments	450	307	607	750	1385	595
Entertainment	200	150	165	450	285	45
Services	150	125	75	365	95	60
Other	166	185	150	255	275	75
Total Monthly Expense	$3,409	$3,104	$3,154	$10,935	$5,515	$2,410
Amount left over	$174.33	−$187.33 Over budget	−$70.67 Over budget	−$101.67 Over budget	$68.33	$2.50

LESSON

16

Choosing and Using a Checking Account

Fitness Focus

EQUIPMENT AND GETTING READY!

Make overhead transparencies of the visuals listed here.

✔ Visual 16.1, *A Hard Lesson for Mr. Smith*

✔ Visual 16.2, *Write a Check*

✔ Visual 16.3, *Electronic Banking*

✔ Visual 16.4, *Check Register*

✔ Visual 16.5, *Check Register Answer Sheet*

All the exercises, readings, and assessment are found in *Shaping Up Your Financial Future Student Workouts.*

✔ Introductory reading for Lesson 16

✔ Exercise 16.1, *Design a Check*

✔ Exercise 16.2, *Using a Checking Account*

✔ Reading 16.1, *About Checking Accounts*

✔ Reading 16.2, *Opening a Checking Account*

✔ Reading 16.3, *Ten Tips for ATM Safety*

✔ Assessment 16.1, *What's Great About Our Checking Accounts!*

LESSON DESCRIPTION AND BACKGROUND

Checking accounts offer a menu of features along with a menu of costs. In this lesson, the students learn the fundamentals of maintaining a checking account by examining electronic banking methods, check writing, and entries in a check register. The students examine the features and costs of a checking account to prepare them for the time when they acquire checking accounts of their own.

This lesson is correlated with national standards for mathematics and economics as well as the national guidelines for personal financial management as shown in Tables 1 through 3 in the front of the book.

ECONOMIC AND PERSONAL FINANCE CONCEPTS

Credit union, savings and loan, checking account, ATM card, debit card, checkbook register

Student Objectives

At the end of this lesson, the student will be able to:

✔ Identify major features, benefits, and costs of checking accounts.

✔ Explain the responsibilities of having a checking account.

✔ Write a check correctly.

✔ Describe ATM cards, debit cards, direct deposit, and automatic withdrawals.

✔ Identify safety precautions when using ATM machines.

135

PARENT CONNECTION

There is no specific family activity for this lesson, but there are activities in *The Parents' Guide to Shaping Up Your Financial Future* that parents may want to use with this lesson. These activities can be found in the "Raising the Bar" section for Theme 5.¹

The Parents' Guide is a tool for reinforcing and extending the instruction provided in the classroom. It includes:

1. Content background in the form of frequently asked questions.

2. Interesting activities that parents can do with their son or daughter.

3. An annotated listing of books and Internet resources related to each theme.

TIME
REQUIRED
2
class periods

Workout

WARM-UP

1. Introduce the lesson by displaying Visual 16.1, *A Hard Lesson for Mr. Smith*. Ask the students if they know the meaning of "overdrawn." Explain that a checking account becomes overdrawn when the owner of the account has written checks for amounts greater than the amount of money available in the checking account.

2. Explain that the bank may have paid Mr. Smith's checks even though he was overdrawn. However, that is unlikely. The likely scenario is that the checks Mr. Smith wrote "bounced." Ask the students what it means to "bounce a check." A "bounced" check is called an *overdraft*. It is a check written for an amount greater than the amount of money in the checking account, and the bank refuses to pay it, and "bounces" it back to the person who tried to cash it. This practice should be strictly avoided. Overdrafts are expensive. The bank will charge a fee, as high as $25.00 or so, for

each overdraft you write. The business to which you wrote the check is also likely to charge a fee. Another very serious consequence is that a bounced check harms your reputation with the person or business you meant to pay.

3. Explain that in this lesson the students will learn the fundamentals of maintaining a checking account. They will research the different types of accounts, the benefits and costs of each account, and the different types of institutions that offer checking accounts.

4. Point out that checking accounts are useful financial tools. A checking account is not usually important to a middle school student, but as soon as he or she gets a job, a checking account is nearly essential. The students should know how to maintain a checking account before they acquire one. This can help them avoid many embarrassing consequences.

EXERCISE

1. All About Checks

a. Ask the students if they have ever received a check as a gift or if they have

ever seen a check. If so, they will likely know what information it contains. Explain that a check is a promise of payment from the check writer to the check receiver. Refer the students to Exercise 16.1, *Design a Check*. Instruct them to reproduce a check in the space provided. When the students have completed the task, display Visual 16.2, *Write a Check*. Instruct the students to compare their version with a real check.

b. Discuss each check symbol and entry as follows:

▲ The upper-left corner includes the name and address of the check writer. Often people have their phone number printed on the check for convenience.

▲ The upper-right corner contains the check number. Check numbers are a way of keeping track of the checks you write.

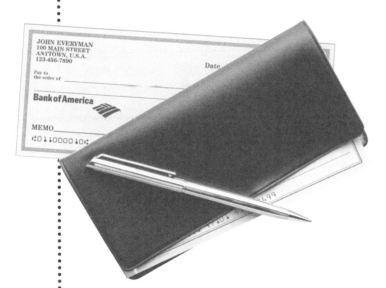

▲ The date line simply shows the date when the check was written. Be sure you have the money in your account to cover the check on the day the check is written. It is unwise to write a check based on a deposit that will take place within the next few days.

▲ The "Pay to the Order" line is for the name of the person or business to be paid. This person or business is entitled to make a claim against your checking account for the dollar amount stated on the check.

▲ The "Pay to the Order" line is followed by a box in which to write the amount of the check in numbers. Write the numbers as close as possible to the dollar sign so that no one can squeeze in additional numbers.

▲ The next line is used to write out the amount of the check in words. This line must agree with the numeric entry above. Always draw a line after having written the amount. In this way, no one can add more to the line.

▲ The name of the bank or financial institution follows under this line. This allows the person to whom the check is written to know where the check writer's account is held.

▲ The "Memo" line allows the check-writer to make a note as to the purpose of the check. The checkwriter can write any notation here. For instance, if the check is being written to the telephone company, this line can be used to write the telephone account number. If the check is being written for cousin Tommy's birthday, the "Memo" line can include a birthday message for Tommy.

▲ The signature line follows the "Memo" line. The signature of the account holder shows that he or she wants the payment made from his or her checking account. It can be compared with the signature card to verify that the account holder wrote the check.

▲ The numbers at the bottom of the check include information about the bank, the checking account number, and the check number. These numbers are scanned when the check is processed to insure accuracy.

c. Refer the students to Reading 16.1, *About Checking Accounts*. When they have completed the reading, ask the following questions:

137

1. **Why would writing checks for payments be safer and more useful than using cash?** *(Cash can be lost or stolen; you can't prove you've made a payment in cash without having a receipt; writing checks helps you keep track of your expenditures; some checking accounts earn interest.)*

2. **What types of costs could you incur by using a checking account?** *(Fees for printed checks, fees for overdrafts [checks written on an overdrawn account], monthly service charges, or a charge for each check you write.)*

d. Refer the students to Reading 16.2, *Opening a Checking Account.* Ask the following questions:

What would be your first step in acquiring a checking account? *(Answers will vary, but the students will likely respond that they would go to the bank. However, as will be explained in the reading, the first step is to choose the institution based on the checking account features offered.)*

Why is completion of a signature card important? *(The signature card can be compared with the signature on the check to assure its authenticity.)*

e. Explain that three types of institutions provide most checking accounts in a community. These include commercial banks, savings and loans, and credit unions. Accounts in these institutions are generally insured through the United States government. Have students identify institutions in the community that offer checking accounts.

f. Explain that banks, savings and loans, and credit unions offer different types of checking accounts with different types of features. One feature of some checking accounts, free checking, is often advertised on bank banners and TV ads. Free checking or other desirable services may require a substantial balance in the account. Some checking accounts may also offer overdraft protection or pay-

ment of interest. Generally, banks, credit unions, and savings institutions offer different checking account packages so that customers can establish accounts that best suit their lifestyles.

g. Refer students back to Reading 16.1, *About Checking Accounts.* Focusing on the features and costs of checking accounts, assign the students to call a bank, credit union, or savings institution in their community and ask about the types of checking accounts they offer. Have them seek answers to the questions posed in the reading. Remind the students that these institutions are not open in the evening, so the calls will have to take place right after school. Explain that they will make a brief report on their findings.

2. Electronic and Online Access to Checking Accounts

a. Point out that writing checks and completing paper deposit tickets are not the only way to access a checking account. Ask the students the following questions:

What is an ATM? *(The students will likely respond that it is a machine located in malls, airports, and banks where customers can withdraw money from their account. While this is true, explain that ATM stands for Automated Teller Machine, and it has several other functions, such as allowing*

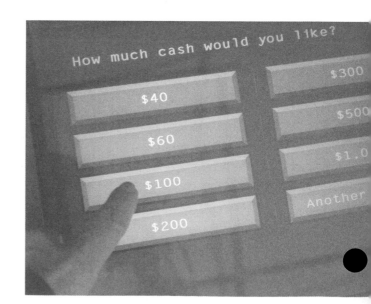

Financial Fitness for Life: Shaping Up Your Financial Future Teacher Guide, ©National Council on Economic Education

the account holder to transfer money from one account to another, to check an account balance, or to deposit money.)

What is an ATM card? *(It is an identification card that allows the holder to withdraw money from his or her account at an ATM. A personal identification number [PIN], along with the card, is required for transactions.)*

b. Explain that the use of an ATM is only one of several electronic banking services. Display Visual 16.3, *Electronic Banking*. Explain each of the electronic methods as follows:

1. ATMs are the electronic service with which students may be most familiar. Explain that these machines can be used at all hours of the day or night. Customers may make deposits to or withdrawals from their accounts, verify their account balances, and transfer money from one account to another. Customers may also use other banks' ATMs, but they should be careful in doing this. Other banks often charge a fee for the use of their machine. Customers should be cautious using ATMs for another reason. Crimes of theft and fraud associated with the use of ATMs have been reported. Use care when you withdraw or deposit cash at an ATM. Refer the students to Reading 16.3, *Ten Tips for ATM Safety*, for additional safety precautions. Instruct the students to share this information with their parents.

2. The debit card is another type of electronic payment method. The card for the ATM is many times the same one used as a debit card. This card is used much like a credit card. The customer makes a purchase, his or her debit card is scanned, the customer inserts the PIN, and a sales slip is given to the customer for signature. Although the debit card is used like a credit card, there is one huge difference. A credit card is a loan the customer takes to pay for the purchase later. A debit card immediately transfers money from your checking account to the merchant's account. Using a debit card is simple, fast, and convenient. However, treat it like cash; if someone gets possession of your card, he or she may be able to make purchases.

3. Ask the students if they've ever watched their parents sit down to pay the bills. Bills for services, such as the telephone, cable TV, and electricity come every month. These transactions can't be handled by debit cards or ATMs, so consumers must write out check after check, pay postage, and make a trip to the post office. However, there is an electronic answer to this problem. Bank customers can use online banking for paying these bills. Online banking is done various ways. One way is to have the financial institution where you have your account pay your regularly scheduled bills electronically from your account. Monthly rent for housing, electric bills, and telephone bills are examples of bills which would be handled by the financial institution. Another form of online banking is where the consumer can make payments electronically. With this type of online banking, the customer can transfer funds from one account to another, pay bills, and see his or her bank statement. A PIN is needed to access the account; an Internet capability is also required.

4. Money that bank customers receive regularly by check can be electronically transferred to the customers' accounts. This service is called direct deposit. People often use this service to deposit their paychecks. Instead of being given a check, the worker gets a confirmation that his or her money has been deposited. There are several advantages to using direct deposits. They save trips to the bank to cash checks; they eliminate the possibility of losing the checks; and the money usually gets into the account sooner.

139

5. There is one very important pitfall to avoid when using electronic banking services. Customers must always remember to write the transaction in their check register. Display Visual 16.4, *Check Register.* Explain that a account holder can keep a running balance of a checking account in the check register. Each time a check is written, the account holder can simply write in the date, check number, to whom the check was written, and the amount of the check. The account holder deducts the amount of the check from the previous balance. This is very convenient because the pad of checks and the check register are contained in the same book. However, with electronic transactions, the check register may not be handy when the transaction occurs. The account holder must remember to note the automatic deposits and withdrawals.

3. Using a Checkbook

a. Refer the students to Exercise 16.2, *Using a Checking Account.* This activity gives the students practice in keeping a checkbook register. The balance at the end of the transaction list is $97.13. When the students complete the exercise, display Visual 16.5, *Answer Sheet* so that the students can check their work. Make sure the students are following the rules for writing checks presented earlier.

b. Explain that if there are errors in the check register, the account holder will find them if he or she is careful to balance the checking account each month. The bank sends a statement each month. The statement shows the balance in the account at the beginning of the monthly cycle. Then it lists each deposit and each check that was sent to the bank for payment. Finally, it provides an ending balance. It is very easy to reconcile a check register with the statement by following the directions on the back of the statement, and it is very important to do so soon after receiving the statement. A bank reconciliation should be completed, generally every month, to make sure that the balance in your account equals the bank's balance for your account. Otherwise, one can easily overdraw an account.

COOL DOWN

1. Ask the students if they think there will come a time when people stop using cash altogether.

Explain that a cashless society has been predicted for a long time; however, most people like to have a little cash in their pockets for emergencies or small purchases. Ask the students what it would take to create a cashless society: what types of banking services would bring it to reality? *(The students should describe ATMs, debit cards, direct deposit, automatic withdrawals, and online banking.)*

2. As a review ask the students to read the *Warm-Up, Fitness Vocabulary, Muscle Developers* and *Showing Your Strength* in *Student Workouts.*

After reading, ask the students the following questions:

Why should one shop for a checking account? *(Because there are many checking account plans that vary in costs and services. One should find the checking account that best meets his or her needs and wants.)*

Why is secrecy important for your PIN and your ATM and debit card? *(Your PIN should never be given to anyone or kept in the same place as your debit or ATM card. Someone who learns your PIN can use your card to access your checking account without your knowledge or permission.)*

Why is it important to keep good records when you have a checking account? *(So you know how much money you have in the account; to avoid overdrawing the account; to develop a good reputation (character); or to avoid maintaining too much money in a non-interest account. Money not needed in the* *checking account can be moved to a savings account that pays interest.)*

Why do financial institutions charge fees for a person to have a checking account? *(It costs the financial institutions to process checks and deposits.)*

Assessment

Instruct the students to use the information they gathered on checking accounts for this assignment. Tell the students that they will act as public relations persons for the financial institution; instruct them to write a public relations advertisement about the institution's services. They should include the institution's features, such as location and banking hours, and the features of the account, such as per-check fees, minimum balances, and so on. Refer them to Assessment 16.1 for the features and costs of checking accounts that should be included in their advertisement.

Other Training Equipment

An annotated bibliography and Internet resource list are available on our web site, **www.ncee.net**, or in *The Parents' Guide to Shaping Up Your Financial Future*.

141

Visual 16.1

A Hard Lesson for Mr. Smith

Banker:

Mr. Smith, your checking account is overdrawn.

Mr. Smith:

How can that be? I still have checks!

Visual 16.2

Write a Check

GRACE OWENS
117 Kennedy Blvd.
Everytown, USA
Telephone 314-100-2394

5392

Date _July 30_ , 20 _02_

Pay to
the order of _Elvis Building Company_ $ _49.03_

Forty nine and 03/100 ——————————————— Dollars

Bank of America
Some City, USA

Sample only. Not negotiable.

MEMO _lumber supplies_   _Grace Owens_

⑆0110000000⑆ 011111111111100⑈ 5392

Financial Fitness for Life: Shaping Up Your Financial Future Teacher Guide, ©National Council on Economic Education

Visual 16.3

Electronic Banking

Electronic banking may sound impersonal, but it's actually a fast and easy way to use banking services. You can:

▲ make deposits

▲ make withdrawals (get cash)

▲ pay loans

▲ pay bills

▲ transfer money between accounts

▲ pay for purchases at the point of sale

▲ check your account status

Electronic banking includes:

▲ Automated Teller Machines (ATMs)

▲ Debit cards

▲ Automatic withdrawals/transfers

▲ Direct deposits

▲ Online banking services

Visual 16.4

Check Register

PLEASE BE SURE TO DEDUCT CHARGES THAT AFFECT YOUR ACCOUNT							BALANCE	
CHECK #	DATE	TRANSACTION DESCRIPTION	WITHDRAWAL/ SUBTRACTIONS	✓ T	FEE IF ANY	DEPOSIT/ ADDITIONS	145	52

Visual 16.5

Check Register Answer Sheet

CHECK #	DATE	TRANSACTION DESCRIPTION	WITHDRAWAL/ SUBTRACTIONS		✓ T	FEE IF ANY	DEPOSIT/ ADDITIONS		BALANCE 145	52
8452	9/4	Gibson's Record Shop new tape	9	88					-9 135	88 64
X	9/8	Deposit					66	95	+66 202	95 59
8453	9/11	Grayson's Service Station oil change	24	50					-24 178	50 09
8454	9/15	Acme Jewelers deposit on class ring	15	00					-15 163	00 09
ATM	9/19	Cash withdrawal	40	00					-40 123	00 09
X	9/22	Deposit					63	88	+63 186	88 97
8455	9/23	Lee Johnson loan	5	00					-5 181	00 97
8456	9/26	American Publishing	13	75					-13 168	75 22
8457	9/27	Neighbor's Store mom's birthday gift	28	63					-28 139	63 59
X	9/29	Deposit					10	00	+10 149	00 59
auto	9/30	Automatic withdrawal auto loan	47	56					-47 102	56 03
svc ch	10/1	Service Charge	4	90					-4 97	90 13

PLEASE BE SURE TO DEDUCT CHARGES THAT AFFECT YOUR ACCOUNT

Financial Fitness for Life: Shaping Up Your Financial Future Teacher Guide, ©National Council on Economic Education

THEME 5

LESSON

17

What Taxes Affect You?

Fitness Focus

EQUIPMENT AND GETTING READY!

Make overhead transparencies of the visuals listed here.

✔ Visual 17.1, *Tax Troubles*

✔ Visual 17.2, *Local Government Provides...*

✔ Visual 17.3, *State Government Provides...*

✔ Visual 17.4, *Federal Government Provides...*

✔ Visual 17.5, *Who Got a "Pizza" My Paycheck?*

✔ Introductory reading for Lesson 17 (*Shaping Up Your Financial Future Student Workouts*)

✔ Reading 17.1, *Is This a Road or a Parking Lot? (Shaping Up Your Financial Future Student Workouts)*

✔ Assessment 17.1, *Where Did the Money Go? (Shaping Up Your Financial Future Student Workouts)*

✔ Supply of sales receipts with sales tax included.

LESSON DESCRIPTION AND BACKGROUND

In a perfect world, we would be provided roads, schools, police, parks, and other public goods and services without the burden of taxation. However, in most cases, government must offer these goods and services, because private industry will not provide them.

Pure public goods and services share two characteristics: *non-exclusion* and *shared consumption*. Non-exclusion refers to the inability to keep people from consuming or benefiting from the good. For instance, it would be impossible to keep people from benefiting from streets and highways. Shared consumption refers to a good or service in which an additional consumer can use the good without additional cost. For example, although the population of the U.S. has grown, our borders have not. Therefore, the costs associated with providing a national defense do not increase just because the number of people to defend increases.

In this lesson, the students observe that they already pay taxes in the form of sales tax, and they will soon be obligated to pay income tax. Students also gain understanding of the goods and services paid for by taxes.

Student Objectives

At the end of this lesson, the student will be able to:

✔ Define and explain income, property, and sales taxes.

✔ Explain what goods and services government provides at the local, state, and federal levels.

✔ Explain why government provides some goods and services, but not others.

147

This lesson is correlated with national standards for mathematics and economics as well as the national guidelines for personal financial management as shown in Tables 1 through 3 in the front of the book.

ECONOMIC AND PERSONAL FINANCE CONCEPTS

Income tax, sales tax, property tax

PARENT CONNECTION

There is no specific family activity for this lesson, but there are activities in *The Parents' Guide to Shaping Up Your Financial Future* that parents may want to use with this lesson. These activities can be found in the "Raising the Bar" section for Theme 5.

The Parents' Guide is a tool for reinforcing and extending the instruction provided in the classroom. It includes:

1. Content background in the form of frequently asked questions.

2. Interesting activities that parents can do with their son or daughter.

3. An annotated listing of books and Internet resources related to each theme.

Workout

WARM-UP

1. Introduce the lesson by displaying Visual 17.1, *Tax Troubles*. Explain that these terms refer to organizations that can be found on the Internet. Ask the students if they have ever heard of any of these organizations and if they can draw any inferences about what these organizations sponsor. They most likely have not heard of these groups, but they might infer that these groups sponsor movements toward tax reform.

2. Point out that many people complain about paying taxes. The organizations listed on the visual are just a few of dozens, maybe hundreds, of web sites advocating everything from paying no taxes to tax reform. Some complaints focus on the level of taxes, while others are concerned with the methods used for taxation. Ask the students what types of complaints or reform ideas they have heard. *(Most students will recognize that people complain that they pay too much in taxes. The informed students may know of suggestions to adopt a proportional income tax or national sales tax as an alternative to our present system.)*

3. Explain that taxation has been around almost as long as civilization. Early emperors and kings demanded tribute from their subjects. The money collected supported the empires and the kingdoms and provided limited defense. Even the Bible refers to taxes in the quotation, "Render unto Caesar what is Caesar's." Define *taxes* as required payments of money to the government. Write the definition on the board.

4. Ask the students what type of taxes they pay. The sales tax would be a tax they all pay unless the state where they live doesn't have a sales tax. Define *sales tax* as a tax paid on items purchased by consumers.

Provide each student with receipts for purchases made locally. Instruct the students to observe the sales tax charged on the receipt. Explain that the sales tax is a percentage of the sale price. For instance, a community may charge four percent sales tax and the state in which that community is located might charge a two percent sales tax, meaning that for every dollar a consumer spends, he or she must pay six cents in tax. Instruct the students to examine the receipts provided. In some cases, the sales tax percentage will be printed on the receipt. Have a student report the percentage shown on a receipt. If none of the receipts indicate the percentage amount,

instruct the students to calculate the percentage charged.

5. Explain that, in addition to sales tax, communities assess *property taxes*. This is a tax on real estate and, sometimes, on personal property such as cars and boats. Some cities and most states have instituted an *income tax*. The federal government also assesses an income tax. This is a tax in which the percentage of tax you pay is based on your level of income.

6. Have the students read the *Warm-Up, Fitness Vocabulary*, *Muscle Developers*, and *Showing Your Strength* of Lesson 17 in *Student Workouts*.

EXERCISE

1. Refer the students to Reading 17.1, *Is This a Road or a Parking Lot?* in *Student Workouts*. Ask the students what their answer is to how the new road will most likely be financed. (*Taxes.*) Ask the students why other methods suggested in the reading would not work. (*Road construction would not be profitable for private industry to provide; voluntary contributions are likely to fall short of the needed money because not everyone would be willing to contribute.*) Ask them how their community pays for new roads. (*Taxes.*)

a. Ask if they can identify any new road construction in their area. Explain that government pays for most roads. Some streets in the community are constructed

and maintained by the local community government. Some larger roads are constructed and maintained by the county or state government. The federal government provides interstate highways.

b. Explain that roads are just one example of government-provided goods and services. Ask the students to brainstorm other goods and services in their community, state, and country that are publicly owned and maintained. Record their answers on the board. (*Answers will vary but could include public libraries, parks, museums, public health clinics or hospitals, police and fire protection, schools, water, sewage, and garbage services. The students are not likely to know which level of government provides the goods and services they have named.*)

2. Explain that governments provide goods and services that are not likely to be provided in any other way. Governments get the money to provide goods and services by requiring citizens to pay taxes.

a. Ask the students to speculate as to which of the goods and services listed are provided by local government. Then display the Visual 17.2, *Local Government Provides…* Help the students

recognize that the number of goods and services provided by local government varies from place to place, but the items on the list are typical of the goods and services provided by local government. Ask the following questions:

▲ **What goods and services are provided within our school?** *(Answers will vary, but guide the students to compile a list similar to the following: teachers, custodial workers, secretaries, books, classrooms, lighting, heat, art supplies, etc.)*

▲ **What parks and recreational programs does our city (or county) provide?** *(Answers will vary, but guide the students to name all local parks, skating rinks, pools, ball fields, etc.)*

▲ **What is needed by our law enforcement programs to perform its responsibilities?** *(Answers will vary, but guide the students to consider police, police cars, police bicycles or horses, courthouses, judges, court clerks, jails, guards, safety and educational programs, such as D.A.R.E., etc.)*

b. Ask the students to suggest goods and services provided by state government. Display Visual 17.3, *State Government Provides…* Begin a discussion of the items on the list by posing the following questions:

▲ **Is anyone acquainted with someone who is currently attending a state college/university? Who is it? Which university does he or she attend?** *(Answers will vary.)*

▲ **Does your acquaintance (relative) have to pay any money to attend the university?** *(The students may or may not be aware that, in most cases, the students are required to pay some amount of money toward their educational costs. Explain that the price the students pay is far lower than the actual cost of the education because the state pays for a good portion of the cost of the students' education.)*

▲ **What state parks have you visited?** *(Answers will vary.)* **What types of services are provided there?** *(Again, answers will vary, but many state parks offer camping grounds, picnic areas, covered shelters, security, and nature programs.)*

c. Ask the students to suggest goods and services provided by the federal government. Display Visual 17.4, *Federal Government Provides…* Explain that some of the federal government's expenditures buy goods and services for citizens. Other federal government expenditures are payments made to individuals to help them through rough times. These payments are called transfer payments. Discuss some of the goods and services and transfer payments on the list by asking the following questions:

▲ **What types of goods and services are included in our national defense system?** *(Lead the students to include in the discussion some large-ticket items, such as wages for military personnel, fighter jets, transport jets, helicopters, tanks, and missiles.)*

▲ **What programs help people through rough times in the lives of their families?** *(Housing programs, food stamps, Medicare, medicaid, social security.)*

▲ **Why does the federal government offer these types of programs?** *(If the students are unclear as to why these programs are offered, explain that one of the goals of the federal government is to provide economic equity. This means that we, as a society, have decided that people should have some of their most important basic wants provided by government if they are having a hard time providing these things for themselves.)*

▲ **What is Social Security and Medicare?** *(Social Security is a federal program to provide the elderly with some retirement income, to assist minor children of a parent who has died, and to assist people living with disabilities. This program is not designed to cover all of the*

150

costs these people may incur, but is considered a supplement to the money saved for retirement, or to assist a family to cope with loss of income due to death or disability. Medicare is a federal health care program for people over the age of 65.)

▲ **Which of these programs do you consider to be among the most important?** *(Answers will vary, but the students should recognize that we have all benefited from national defense and interstate highways. The students may also know people who are receiving Social Security or have received "safety net" assistance, such as housing assistance or unemployment compensation.)*

3. Remind the students that they regularly pay sales tax. However, in a few years, they will be paying income taxes. *Income taxes* are taxes on income, both earned income (salaries, wages, tips, commissions) and unearned income (interest from savings accounts, dividends if you hold stock).

a. Explain to the students that when they are acccpted for employment, their first official tax-related duty will be to fill out a *Form W-4*. This form will tell your employer how much money he or she should withhold from your paycheck for income tax. The withheld tax is based on an estimate of the income taxes you will owe. What you will owe is based, in part, on how many people rely on you for their

support. These are your *dependents*. If you claim zero dependents, your employer will withhold the largest tax allowable. If you claim one dependent, your employer will withhold a smaller amount of your money. You may not claim more than one dependent if you have no one financially dependent on you, other than yourself. And you may not claim yourself if your parents or guardians claim you as one of their dependents.

b. Point out that *withholding* is the money that is withheld, sent to the government, and credited to the employee's tax bill. This helps the employee "save" money for taxes. Explain that sometimes employees withhold a little more than is required. This better assures the employees that their taxes are covered for the year, leaving a refund to be returned. On the other hand, withholding more than is required deprives the employee of money he or she could be spending or saving during the year and gives "Uncle Sam" an interest-free loan.

4. Display Visual 17.5, *Who Got a "Pizza" My Paycheck?* Explain that it often comes as a surprise to many new workers when they get their first paychecks and discover they have not received all of the money they expected. Point out that the taxes withheld are for various purposes. Local, state, and federal taxes pay for the goods and services already discussed. FICA, a tax established by the Federal Insurance Contributions Act, pays into the funds established for Social Security and Medicare. The benefits of these taxes occur now and in the future.

Financial Fitness for Life: Shaping Up Your Financial Future Teacher Guide, ©National Council on Economic Education

COOL DOWN

Explain that in this lesson, the students have learned about the taxes they currently pay, and taxes they will pay in just a few years. They have also learned the reasons why taxes are important in our society. Ask the following questions:

▲ **What are taxes?** *(Taxes are required payments of money to the government.)*

▲ **What types of taxes do you pay currently?** *(Sales tax, in some states, and possibly income taxes.)*

▲ **What are income taxes?** *(Taxes on both earned and unearned income.)*

▲ **What is earned income?** *(Money received in salaries, wages, tips, commissions.)*

▲ **What goods and services do local taxes provide?** *(Accept a few answers, such as local roads, police, parks, and so on.)*

▲ **What goods and services do state taxes provide?** *(Accept a few answers, such as state roads, state parks, state courts, prisons, and so on.)*

▲ **What goods and services do federal taxes provide?** *(Accept a few answers, such as national defense, the space program, transportation, and so on.)*

▲ **Why must governments provide these goods and services?** *(Private industry is not likely to provide these types of goods and services because it is difficult to receive payment in return for their use.)*

Assessment

Refer the students to Assessment 17.1, *Where Did the Money Go?* in *Student Workouts.*

The answers are as follows: *1. Personal information, such as the employee's name and social security number, are reported along with the number of dependents to estimate the amount of withholding. 2. The students should respond with any of the goods and services provided by the state, such as state universities, highways & bridges, prisons, and so on. 3. The students should respond with the goods, services, and transfer payments provided by the federal government, such as national defense, transportation, energy programs, and so on. 4. The money collected through FICA deductions goes toward the support of Social Security and Medicare. Federal income tax pays for other government-provided goods and services.*

Other Training Equipment

An annotated bibliography and Internet resource list are available on our web site, **www.ncee.net**, or in *The Parents' Guide to Shaping Up Your Financial Future.*

Visual 17.1

Tax Troubles

Bleed the Beast

Freedom Tax School

Income Tax Freedom

Inform America

Passport Society

Visual 17.2

Local Government (City and/or County) Provides...

▲ Local roads, signals, and signs

▲ Schools

▲ Libraries

▲ Community parks

▲ Streetlights and sidewalks

▲ Police and fire protection

▲ City courts

▲ City jails

▲ Health clinics and hospitals (sometimes)

Visual 17.3

State Government Provides...

▲ State highways and bridges

▲ State colleges/universities

▲ Assistance with funding local schools

▲ State police and highway patrols

▲ State prisons

▲ State courts

▲ State parks

▲ Job training programs

▲ Health care and state hospitals

Visual 17.4

Federal Government Provides...

Goods and Services

▲ National defense
▲ Veterans' programs
▲ Military and economic assistance to other countries
▲ Foreign embassies
▲ Agricultural programs
▲ Transportation
▲ Assistance to elementary and secondary schools
▲ Job training programs
▲ Financial assistance for college students
▲ The space program
▲ Energy programs
▲ Scientific research
▲ Prisons
▲ Federal law enforcement (the FBI)
▲ Tax collection
▲ National Parks
▲ Federal Reserve System/Currency

Transfer Payments

▲ Food stamps
▲ Housing payments for the poor
▲ Social Security and Medicare
▲ Health care for the poor (Medicaid)

Visual 17.5

Who Got a "Pizza" My Paycheck?

You've landed your first job. The local pizza place will pay you $5.25 per hour, plus tips. You have agreed to work 25 hours per week. Quick, do the math!

In addition to your first-week's wages, you also earned $150 in tips. Between wages and tips, you have earned $281.25 for only one week's work. You are in the money!

That was the good news. Now, here's the bad news. You, like every other worker, must have some of your money withheld to pay taxes. This is how it breaks down:

First week's wages:. $131.25
First week's tips:. 150.00
Total wages and tips **$281.25**

Federal Tax Withheld
(one exemption claimed on Form W-4):. $26.00
State Taxes (amount varies from state to state): . . . 5.25
Local Taxes (amount varies from place to place):. . . 1.28
Social Security Tax Withheld:. 17.46
Medicare Tax: 4.08
Total deductions: **$54.07**
Net Pay: (What you take home.) **$227.18**

Source: Internal Revenue Service (**www.irs.gov/prod/taxi/learninglab/payday/whogetsdude.html**)

NOTES